NORWEGIAN HOME COMPANION

Merry Xmas 1999
To Paula + George
May you enjoy this book as much
as we did.
Too bad your parents couldn't
read this — however, they probably
heard them all before.

Jack + Judy

Ole & Lena

Red Stangland's

NORWEGIAN
· HOME ·
COMPANION

BARNES
&NOBLE
BOOKS
NEW YORK

This edition published by Barnes & Noble, Inc.,
by arrangement with Red Stangland.

ISBN 0-88029-521-X *casebound*
ISBN 1-56619-815-1 *paperback*

Printed and bound in the United States of America

MC 12
MP 9 8 7 6 5 4 3

TABLE OF CONTENTS

INTRODUCTION

Telling ethnic jokes can sometimes be a hazard to your health. In the case of Norwegian jokes, it can just as likely be the beginning of a friendship. Strange? Yes, it is still a mystery why Norwegians and other Scandinavians have a strong tolerance for jokes on their identities. For some reason, they don't seem to feel that the prankish dumb guy gags about Ole, Lena, and their friends can possibly apply to THEM. Norwegians in particular love to spin these yarns, with stress on the accents where "J" becomes "Y", and "TH" becomes "D," as in: Ole says, "I think I vill yust go down to da river and vatch de fish yump around."

Even noted author of Lake Wobegon fame, Garrison Keillor, has high praise for Ole & Lena tales and other Norwegian jokes. He calls author Red Stangland the "Tolstoy and Einstein" of Norwegian humor. In fact, several of Red's jokes were used in Keillor's recent volume, "WLT, A Radio Romance."

So, help yourself to a thousand laughs in a book that will cheer you up no matter what. And you will never again be lonely, because this is Red Stangland's NORWEGIAN HOME COMPANION.

The editors

AUTHOR'S PROFILE

Author Red Stangland has made Norwegian jokes into an art form highlighted by the personifications of Norseness, Ole and Lena. Red, a career radio broadcaster never met a Norwegian joke he didn't like. If he like one well enough, it goes into one of his books. Red (who is actually white haired) travels on the "rubber chicken" circuit frequently, delivering his humorous monologues about Ole & Sven, Lars, Knute, Helga, and of course, Lena. Many of his performances are in Lutheran Churches and Sons of Norway lodges, so it shows that his fellow Scandinavians are quite forgiving. In fact, Red was President of his local Sons of Norway a few years ago. Red and his wife (a Dane) have a daughter, Susan, and a son, Jeff. Red and Norma live in Sioux Falls, South Dakota, where you may send your favorite joke if you feel so inspired. The mailing address is: Box 1554, Sioux Falls, S.D. 57101. You may even see your joke in a future book by this Scandinavian One-Liner King, whose inspiration and good friend is noted comic, Henny Youngman. If you ever meet Red in person, you may discover he is a veritable Vesuvius of Norwegian jokes and will swap jokes with you any time, any day.

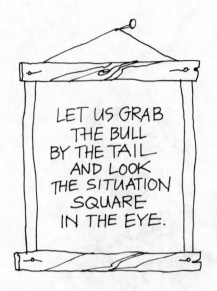

ONE

Original THE NORWEGIAN JOKES

NORWEGIAN: Did you ever eat lutefisk?
DANE: No . . . but I think I stepped in some one time.

■   ■   ■   ■

The Swedes are proud of their new zoo.
They built a fence around Norway.

■   ■   ■   ■

Two Norwegians were talking in the park when a bird splattered one of them on the head. Eyeing the mess, the victim's companion offered to go get some toilet paper. "Von't do no good," said the messed-up one, "by the time you get back, dat bird will be four miles avay."

Two Norwegians dressed a hog in overalls and placed it between them in their pick-up truck as they crossed the Swedish border. Their motive was to avoid paying a special livestock tax. The border guard eyed the trio, asking their names. "Ole Johnson." "Knute Johnson." Then, the hog: "Oink." Passing them on, the guard remarked to his assistant, "I've seen some bad looking people in my time, but that Oink Johnson has got to be the ugliest Norwegian I've ever seen."

■   ■   ■   ■

What do you get when you cross a Norwegian with a flower?
—A Blooming Idiot!

■   ■   ■   ■

How did the Norwegian get pregnant?
He went out with a telephone operator and she reversed the charge.

■   ■   ■   ■

Norwegian plumber's dream:
Fixing Farrah's fawcett . . .
or Olivia Newton's John.

Why did the Norwegian sleep under an oil tank? Because he wanted to get up oily.

. . . .

Two Norwegians went with a pair of young ladies for a ride in the country. An hour later as Lars and Ole were trudging back to town on foot, Lars remarked, "Next time ve tell some girls to either cooperate or get out and valk . . . ve better make sure ve got our own car."

. . . . .

The phone company is going to pick a new emergency number to replace 911.
Most Norwegians can't find ELEVEN on the dial.

. . . .

A Norwegian was having trouble picking a name for his new daughter. "I have trouble saying 'Yenevieve,' so I think ve'll call her Wiolet."

. . . . .

A Norwegian thought diarrhea was hereditary because he discovered it in his genes (jeans).

What's the best thing to come out
of Norway recently?
An empty boat.

■ ■ ■ ■

There's a new Norwegian insurance policy.
It's called "My Fault Insurance."

■ ■ ■ ■

Ole, the Norwegian hired man, was called into the bedroom of the lady of the house. "Ole," she said, "take off my dress." Ole complied. "Now, Ole . . . take off my stockings." Ole did. "Now, Ole take off my brassiere and panties." Again Ole obeyed. "Now, Ole," said the Boss' wife, "next time you go into town, you wear your OWN clothes."

■ ■ ■ ■

A Norwegian carrying a rock, a chicken and a pail paused at a closed gate. He asked a Norwegian farm girl if she'd open the gate. She declined, saying, "You might make love to me." Snorted the Norsky, "How could I make love to you with a rock, a chicken and a pail in my arms?" "Vell," said the girl, "you could set the chicken down, put the pail over it, and then set the rock on top of the pail."

4

HOW TO MAKE YOUR OWN NORWEGIAN FLASHLIGHT

1. TAKE THE CENTER TUBE FROM A ROLL OF TOILET PAPER.

2. USE CELLOPHANE TAPE TO BIND 12 PAPER MATCHES TO THE UPPER RIM OF TUBE.

3. TAPE STRIKER STRIP NEAR BOTTOM OF TUBE ALONG WITH STARTER MATCH.!

A Norwegian lady quit using the pill.
It kept falling out.

■ ■ ■ ■

LADY (attending the Olympics):
"Are you a Pole Vaulter?"
NORWEGIAN: "No . . . I'm a Norwegian . . .
and my name ain't Valter."

■ ■ ■ ■

A TV network is planning a two hour special.
A Norwegian will attempt to count to 100.

■ ■ ■ ■

WOMAN: Oh, my goodness . . . my husband is
driving in the driveway!
NORWEGIAN: I better get outta here. Vhere is
your back door?
WOMAN: We don't have a back door.
NORWEGIAN: Vell, vhere vould you like vun?

■ ■ ■ ■

Did you hear about the intelligent Norwegian?
It was just a rumor.

A NORWEGIAN MOTHER WRITING
TO HER SON

My dear son:

Yust a few lines to let yew know I am still alive. I am writing this letter slowly becoss I know you can't read fast.

You won't know the house when yew come home. Ve have moved.

Ve had a lot of trouble moving . . . especially the bed. The man vouldn't let us take it in the taxi. It maybe vouldn't have been so bad if your father hadn't been in it at the time.

Speaking of your father, he has a fine new yob. He has 500 men under him! (He cuts grass at the cemetery.)

Your sister got herself engaged last veek. Her boy friend gave her a beautiful ring with three stones missing.

Our neighbors are now raising pigs. Ve yust got vind of it this morning.

I suppose you didn't know I got my appendix out and a dish washer put in.

Ve found a vash machine in our new house . . . but it doesn't vork so good. Last veek I put in four shirts, pulled the chain and ve hasn't seen the shirts since.

Your sister Ingeborg had a baby yesterday. I haven't heard if it is a boy or a girl. So I can't say yet if you are an aunt or an uncle.

Uncle Thorvald vent to Minneapolis to vork in a bloomer factory. Ve hear he is pulling down 75 a week.

Your Aunt Katrina got a yob in St. Paul vorking in a factory, too. I'm sending her some clean underwear as she says she has been in the same shift since she got there.

Your father didn't have too much to drink at Christmas. I put some castor oil in his whiskey and it kept him going until New Years.

I vent to the doctor on Thursday. Your pa came with me. The Doctor put a glass tube in my mouth and said to keep it shut for ten minutes. Later on, your pa asked to buy it from him.

It vas so vindy last veek! On Monday it was so vindy, one of our chickens laid the same egg four times.

I must close now . . . there's a big sale down town and vomen's bloomers are half off.

Your loving Mother

p.s. I vas going to send you $10 but I already sealed the enveloped.

The Norwegians have invented a new parachute. Opens on impact.

■　■　■　■

Why do Norwegian dogs have flat noses? From chasing parked cars.

■　■　■　■

Why don't Norwegian mothers nurse their babies?
—Because it is so painful when they boil the nipple.

■　■　■　■

A Norwegian applied for a job at the Chicago police department. He was given test after test, but could pass none of them. Desiring to have a Norwegian in the department, as a member of a minority, the Police captain decided to try one more test . . . this one with only one question, "Who shot Lincoln?" The Norwegian answered, "I don't know." "Look," said the Captain, "take this question home and study it. Maybe when you come back tomorrow you'll know the answer." That night, the Norwegian's friends asked him if he got the job. "I tink I might have," said the Norwegian. "Dey got me vorking on a murder case already."

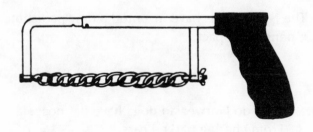

Norwegian Chain Saw

A Norwegian was brought to the hospital with severe facial burns. Seems he had been bobbing for French Fries.

■　■　■　■

Several Norwegian farmers from Minnesota, dissatisfied with low farm prices, decided to march on Washington. At last report, they were 15 miles south of Seattle.

■　■　■　■

Two Norwegians were trying to train their Bird Dog. Said Nels: "Trow him up yust vunce more, Ole; an' if he don't fly dis time, yust shoot him."

The Norwegian was searching frantically for a half dollar when his friend strolled by.

"Where'd ya lose it?" asked the friend.

"Over dere by my car," answered the Norwegian.

"Well, why don't you do your looking over by your car?"

"Because," said the Norsky, "da light is much better here."

■ ■ ■ ■

Famous inventions: The Swedes invented the toilet seat. Twenty years later, the Norwegians invented the hole in it.

■ ■ ■ ■

A fellow in our hometown is starting a new business. He applies black paint on cement blocks and sells them to Norwegians as bowling balls.

■ ■ ■ ■

A Norwegian decided to drive to Omaha to see his cousin. About 20 miles from his destination, he saw a sign, "OMAHA LEFT." So he turned around and went back home.

Did you hear about the Norwegian
who could count to 10?
No?
Would you believe FIVE?

■　■　■　■

A Norwegian went on an elephant hunt, but was forced to turn back because he developed a hernia from carrying the decoy.

■　■　■　■

A Norwegian girl considered getting an abortion because she didn't think the baby was hers.

■　■　■　■

How do you hide money from a Norwegian?
Place it under a soap dish.

■　■　■　■

A Norwegian went to his Doctor for a physical, complaining about his sex life. The Doc told him to walk ten miles a day, then call him on the phone. A week later, the Norwegian telephoned his Doctor. "How's your sex life," inquired the Doc. "What sex?" blurted the Norwegian. "I'm seventy miles from home."

Why does it take two Norwegians to make chocolate chip cookies?
One to mix the batter
and one to squeeze the rabbit.

• • • •

A Norwegian decided to get a vasectomy because he didn't want any more grandchildren.

• • • •

A Norwegian girl competed with a French girl and an English girl in the Breast Stroke division of an English Channel swim competition. The French girl came in first, the English girl second. The Norwegian girl reached shore completely exhausted. After being revived with blankets and coffee, she remarked, "I don't vant to complain, but I tink those other two girls used their arms."

• • • •

A Norwegian was fired at the local packing plant . . . for putting brains in the Polish sausage.

• • • •

What is two miles long and has an IQ of 6?
A Sons of Norway parade.

Did you hear about the Norwegian who broke his
shoulder during a milk drinking contest?
A cow fell on him.

. . . .

Crop scientists have come up with a new strain
known as "Norwegian Oats."
They are tall, light colored and empty headed.

. . . .

A Norwegian appeared with five other men in a rape case
police line-up. As the victim entered the room, the Norwegian blurted, "Yep . . . that's her!"

. . . .

The Norwegian government has been having
problems with their space program.
Their astronaut keeps falling off the kite.

. . . .

Ever wonder who invented streaking?
It was a Norwegian who mistook Ben Gay
for Preparation H.

Ole Swenson was a painter. He had finished painting all the bedrooms upstairs and was to come back the next day and paint the downstairs rooms for Inga Olson. In the meantime, that evening, her husband Lars came home a little tipsy, and while disrobing for bed, caught his foot in his pants leg and put his hand on the wall to steady himself. Of course he left a big smear.

Next day, Ole came to continue painting the downstairs. Inga met him at the door and said, "Ole, come up to the bedroom and see where my husband put his hand last night." Ole said, "No vay, Mrs. Olson. I came here to paint . . . not to fool around!"

■　■　■　■

Last winter ten Norwegians were seen pushing a house down the street. They were trying to get the furnace started.

■　■　■　■

Ole was staggering home from the tavern one night, weaving from side to side. The Lutheran minister saw him and in a Good Samaritan impulse, offered to guide Ole to his home. As they approached the house, Ole suggested that the minister go inside for a moment. He explained, "I vant Lena to see who I have been out vith."

What do you call a 35 year old Norwegian
in the third grade?
A genius.

■ ■ ■ ■

When the Norwegian accidentally lost 50 cents in the outhouse, he immediately threw in his watch and billfold. He
explained, "I'm not going down dere yust for 50 cents."

■ ■ ■ ■

Two Norwegians brought their wives on a trip to America.
They were soon trying to adopt American customs . . . in
fact, Lars even suggested to Ole that they swap partners
"like they do in America." So they did. About 11:30 that
night, Lars asked Ole . . . "I vonder how da vimmen folks
are getting along."

■ ■ ■ ■

During the big flood around Fargo in 1975, several Norwegians waited by the river bank with toothbrushes. They
were waiting for the Crest.

■ ■ ■ ■

Then there was the Norwegian who noticed the sign,
"Wet Pavement" . . . so he did.

So, THAT'S the difference between Danes and Norwegians?

A Norwegian came home one day and shot his dog. When a neighbor expressed surprise, the Norwegian explained, "Some vun phoned me up and said my vife was fooling around vith my best friend."

. . . .

Why do Norwegians smile when it lightnings?
They think they're getting their picture taken.

. . . .

A Norwegian moved to Ireland and joined the IRA. His first assignment was to blow up a bus. But he failed because he burned his mouth on the exhaust pipe.

. . . .

A Norwegian race driver entered the Indianapolis 500. He had to make 75 pit stops . . . 3 for gas and oil and tire changes and 72 to ask directions.

. . . .

A Norwegian decided to take up hunting. So, off into the woods he went . . . when suddenly a beautiful blonde appeared. "Are you game?" asked the Norsky. "I certainly am," purred the blonde. So the Norwegian shot her.

Why is there always a garbage can present at a Norwegian wedding?
To keep the flies off the bride.

. . . .

A Norwegian received a pair of water skis for his birthday.
He went crazy looking for a slope on the lake.

. . . .

Ole and Lena got married. On their honeymoon trip, they were nearing Minneapolis when Ole put his hand on Lena's knee. Giggling, Lena said, "Ole, you can go farther if you vant to." So Ole drove on to Duluth.

. . . .

There's a new Norwegian drink that is becoming popular, a mixture of vodka and prune juice. It's called a "Pile Driver."

. . . .

What do you find on the bottom of cola bottles in Norway?
The inscription "Open other end."

Two elderly Norwegian ladies in a nursing home decided one day to go "streaking" in order to relieve the monotony. As they paraded down the hallway in their all-together, two old codgers looked up from their wheelchairs. "What was that?" queried one of the old fellows. "Dunno . . . guess it was a couple of women." "What were they wearing?" asked the first. "Dunno," came the answer, "but whatever it was . . . it sure needed ironing."

■　■　■　■

What was the tragedy concerning the four
Norwegians who drowned in the station wagon
that went into the river?
The wagon could have held 6.

■　■　■　■

A great medical breakthrough was recently reported. The Norwegians have now performed the first successful hernia transplant.

■　■　■　■

Two Norwegians at the funeral of their friend Nels. "He sure looks good," said one.
"He should," remarked the other, "he yust got out of the hospital."

A Norwegian stopped in at a bait shop
and inquired as to the cost of worms.
"One dollar for all you need," said the proprietor.
"O.K." answered the Norwegian.
"Give me two dollars worth."

• • • •

We heard about a Norwegian who wanted to be
a stud. He had himself strapped to a snow tire.

• • • •

Two Norwegians from Minnesota went fishing in Canada.
They caught one fish. When they got back, one of the
Norwegians said, "The vay I figure our expenses, dat fish
cost us $400." "Vell," said the other Norwegian, "at dat
price, it's a good ting ve didn't catch any more."

• • • •

Two Norwegians bought a truck and went into the hay
business. They travelled to Nebraska, buying hay for $1 a
bale . . . then hauled it back to South Dakota where they
sold it for $1 a bale. After a month or so, they did a little
figuring and found out they were losing money. "Vell,
dere's only vun ting to do," said one of the Norwegians.
"Ve'll yust have to get us a bigger truck,"

What happened after the Norwegian lost
a $50 bet on a TV football game?
He lost another $50 on the instant replay.

■ ■ ■ ■

Who discovered Norway?
The Roto Rooter man.

■ ■ ■ ■

Who invented the Limbo?
A Norwegian trying to sneak under
a pay toilet door.

■ ■ ■ ■

What's black and blue and lies on the sidewalk?
The guy who tells too many Norwegian stories.

■ ■ ■ ■

Ole was seeing his doctor for a physical. The doctor tried
to give Ole a tactful message about his health.
DOCTOR: I'm afraid I can't do much in the way of treat-
ment right now due to overindulgence in alcohol . . . in
other words, drinking.
OLE: Vell, ven you sober up, let me know and I'll come
back and see you.

Norwegian High Rise

Two Norwegians were trying to get a mule into the barn but its ears were too long. One Norwegian suggested raising the barn. The other one thought they should dig a trench. "No, you dummy," exploded the first, "it's the ears that are too long, not the legs."

．　．　．　．

TORVALD: How do you recognize Ronald McDonald in a nudist camp?
LARS: By da sesame seeds on his buns.

．　．　．　．

LENA: Ole, if I die first, vill you promise to ride to da cemetery vid my mudder?
OLE: Vell, I s'pose I can. But, I'll tell you . . . it vill ruin my whole day!

．　．　．　．

On a recent charter plane trip from Minneapolis to Norway, the pilot was having difficulty maintaining the stability of his 747 jet. He learned from his co-pilot that a large bunch of Norwegians were aboard and they were creating quite a ruckus . . . imbibing a few spirits and running around the plane. So the co-pilot volunteered to go back to see if he could quiet them down. Shortly, the pilot was pleased to note the plane had settled down smoothly and he was able to resume his course. When the co-pilot returned, the pilot asked how he managed to quiet down all those Norwegians. "It was easy," he said, "I just opened the rear hatch and told them there was free lutefisk in the basement."

.   .   .   .

Why does it cost $4 for a Norwegian to get a haircut?
One dollar per side.

.   .   .   .

What did the Norwegian call his mixture of prune juice and 7-Up?
"Hurry up."

.   .   .   .

1st NORSKEY: What's in the sack?
2nd NORSKY: Chickens.
1st NORSKEY: How many?
2nd NORSKY: If you can guess,
I'll give you both of dem.

.   .   .   .

Who was the most famous Norwegian inventor?
Henry Fjord.

Norwegian Tying His Shoe

How do you identify the bride at a Norwegian wedding?
She's the one with the braided armpits.

■   ■   ■   ■

How do you break a Norwegian's finger?
Punch him in the nose.

■   ■   ■   ■

What is a big awkward animal with a trunk?
A Norwegian on vacation.

■   ■   ■   ■

What did the Norwegian call his pet Zebra?
"Spot."

Describe a Norwegian marriage proposal.
"You're going to have a WHAT?"

■ ■ ■ ■

How do they thin out the Norwegian population
in Seattle?
They just throw a handful of coins out on the freeway.

■ ■ ■ ■

We heard of a Norwegian who was so dumb he thought
"innuendo" was the Italian word for Preparation H.

■ ■ ■ ■

Describe a Norwegian Color TV.
A keyhole into the next apartment.

■ ■ ■ ■

What has an IQ of 104?
Six Norwegians.

■ ■ ■ ■

What did the Norwegian say when he saw
his first pizza?
"Who trew up on da lefse?"

The Lutheran minister was chagrined because the church board denied his request for a chandelier for the church. When pressed for the reasons, the chairman explained to the preacher: "Vell, for vun ting . . . da secretary can't spell it. For anudder, nobody knows how to play it, so dat would be a vaste of money. And anudder ting . . . if ve are going to spend any money, it should be for a light over the pulpit so you can see better."

■ ■ ■ ■

A Norwegian landed a job in a lumber yard. The first day they loaded 2 by 4's from a truck into a storage building. The foreman noticed that while the other men were carrying 4 timbers at a time, the Norwegian only carried one. When he politely asked the Norwegian why, the Norwegian snorted, "I sure can't help it if dose odder guys are too lazy to make more trips."

■ ■ ■ ■

Ole got into a lot of trouble recently at the Minneapolis-St. Paul International airport. He was walking through the terminal when he spotted his old friend, Jack Trygstad.
Ole made his big mistake when he shouted across the terminal, "HI, JACK!"

Who was the dumbest Norwegian?
The one who thought Einstein was "one beer."

■ ■ ■ ■

What are the three shortest books?
1. Book of Italian victories in WW II.
2. Irish book of etiquette.
3. Norwegian book of knowledge.

■ ■ ■ ■

What did the Norwegian call his cocktail
of Vodka and Milk of Magnesia?
"A Phillips Screwdriver."

■ ■ ■ ■

Why don't they allow Norwegians to swim
in Lake Superior?
Because they leave a ring.

■ ■ ■ ■

What happened to the Norwegian who ate the
Gammelost? (Old cheese)
They tipped him over 4 times on Halloween.

A German, an Italian and a Norwegian were trying to get into the stadium at the World Olympics at Montreal, but the seats were all sold out. The enterprising German stripped down to his shorts and undershirt, picked up a cane fishing pole in a nearby alley, and marched right in, stating boldly, "Heinrich Schneider, Germany, Pole Vault."

Noting the successful ploy, the Italian took off his outer garments, grabbed a large round stone, then just as boldly strode in the gate, announcing, "Pasquale Galento, Italy, Shot Put."

Not to be outdone, the Norwegian took off all but his BVD's, went into a nearby hardware store where he purchased some barbed wire. As he approached the gate the Norwegian spoke out confidently, "Hjalmar Olson, Norway, fencing."

■ ■ ■ ■

Define: "Dope ring."
Six Norwegians in a circle.

■ ■ ■ ■

A Norwegian was strolling through the farm yard one day when he gazed down to find himself ankle deep in manure.
"Good heavens," he exclaimed, "I'm MELTING!"

Two Norwegians Walking Abreast

When Ole's mother-in-law died, he and Lena were discussing what kind of tombstone to get for her.
Said Ole, "Vell, I tink ve should get vun dat is good and heavy."

. . . .

WOMAN: I was just raped by a Norwegian.
POLICEMAN: How do you know he was Norwegian?
WOMAN: I had to show him how.

A Norwegian took a trip to Fargo, North Dakota. While in a bar, an Indian on the next stool spoke to the Norwegian in a friendly manner. "Look," he said, "let's have a little game. I'll ask you a riddle. If you can answer it, I'll buy YOU a drink. If you can't then you buy ME one. OK?" "Yah, dat sounds purty good," said the Norwegian. Said the Indian, "My father and mother had one child. It wasn't my brother. It wasn't my sister. Who was it?" The Norwegian scratched his head and finally said, "I give up. Who vas it?" "It was ME," chortled the Indian. So the Norwegian paid for the drinks. Back in Sioux Falls the Norwegian went into a bar and spotted one of his cronies, Sven Sandvik. "Sven," he said, "I got a game. If you can answer a question, I'll buy you a drink. If you can't YOU buy ME vun. Fair enough?" "Fair enough," said Sven. "Ok . . . my father and mudder had vun child. It vasn't my brudder. It vasn't my sister. Who vas it?" "Search me," said Sven. "I give up. Who was it?" Said the Norwegian, "It vas some Indian up in Fargo, North Dakota."

■　■　■　■

Erickson the Swede was new on the police force. One day while investigating a dead horse found on the street, he commenced filling out the required report. When he came to the blank: "Location of incident," Erickson scratched his head trying to figure out how to spell "Montmorency Avenue." So, to simplify things for himself, he dragged the horse around the corner to Elm Street.

32

OLE: My car is broke down, so I'm wondering if you could put me up for the night?
FARMER: Well, yes; but you'll have to sleep with my son.
OLE: Darn it all. I'm in the wrong joke.

■ ■ ■ ■

Ole and Lars were going ice fishing. It took them three hours just to dig out enough ice to get their boat in the water.

■ ■ ■ ■

Ole called his local TV station and asked to speak to the weather reporter. "Dis is Ole," he said, "and I yust vant to comment on your vedder report last night ven you predicted 'partly cloudy.' I vant you to know I yust scooped up about 14 inches of 'partly cloudy.' "

■ ■ ■ ■

Ole and Lena were visiting the National Museum in Copenhagen, Denmark. Ole accidentally brushed his elbow against a vase and sent it crashing to the floor where it shattered. An attendant rushed up, exclaiming, "That vase was 2,000 years old."
"Dat's good," said Ole. "I'm sure glad it vasn't a NEW VUN."

Why did the Norwegian freeze to death?
Because he went to the drive-in movie to see
"Closed for the Winter."

. . . .

Difference between "Uff Da" and "Fee Da."
Uff Da . . . dropping a sack of garbage.
Fee Da . . . getting your hand in it.

. . . .

A Norwegian nurse was asked why she had a rectal
thermometer behind her ear.
"My goodness," she exclaimed, "now I remember
where I mislaid that ball point pen."

. . . .

Ole was getting weight conscious. He remarked,
"I used to pinch an inch.
Now I have to grab a SLAB!"

. . . .

Ole says, "Early in our marriage, Lena and I made an
agreement that every week we would go out for a nice
dinner, a little candlelight, a little wine.
She goes Tuesdays and I go Thursdays."

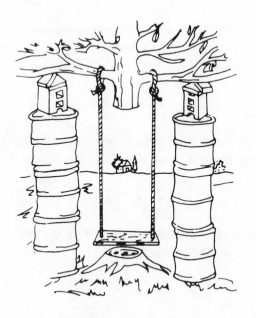

Norwegian Swing

Ole was working as a carpet layer. One day he was installing a carpet for Mrs. Tenneboe. Just as he was finishing up the job, Ole noticed a lump right in the middle of the carpet. He reached in his pocket and couldn't find his cigarettes, so he assumed he had accidentally dropped them where the lump was. So, Ole resourcefully took his hammer and beat down the lump so flat that nobody would notice it was there. Just as he had it nice and smooth, Mrs. Tenneboe walked in and said, "Ole, have you seen anything of my pet parakeet?"

Why were wheelbarrows invented?
To teach the Norwegians to walk
on their hind legs.

. . . .

There once was a Norwegian who, in a rage,
flung himself upon the floor. And missed.

. . . .

Two Norwegians opened a bank. After loaning out all the
money, they skipped town.

. . . .

There was a Norwegian so lazy that he
married a pregnant woman.

. . . .

Why do flies have wings?
So they can beat the Norwegians
to the garbage cans.

. . . .

A Norwegian fox became caught in a trap. It chewed off
three of its feet only to find out it was still caught.

What is the Norwegian national anthem?
"Shoo Fly Don't Bother me."

. . . .

What is a Norwegian shishkabob?
A flaming arrow through a garbage can.

. . . .

A Minneapolis family discovered a nest of skunks under their house. After several attempts to get rid of the little stinkers had failed, they decided to ask some Norwegians down the street to bring some lutefisk to put under the house. The skunks left, all right. But then their problem was to get rid of the Norwegians.

. . . .

A Swede and a Norwegian went up in a plane together. When the plane developed engine trouble, the two bailed out in parachutes. The Swede reached the ground in a matter of about a minute. But the Norwegian got lost and didn't get down until a half hour later.

. . . .

Recently we heard about a Norwegian bookkeeper who absconded with the Accounts Payable.

Give an example of gross ignorance.
"144 Norwegians."

■　■　■　■

Describe a Norwegian compass.
A small mirror to show who's lost.

■　■　■　■

Why does it take 5 Norwegians to paint a house?
You need one to hold the brush
and 4 to turn the house.

■　■　■　■

A Norwegian answers the phone at 3 a.m. Wrong number, so the caller apologizes.
"Dats OK," said the Norwegian. "I had to get up
to answer the phone anyvay."

■　■　■　■

MARRIAGE LICENSE CLERK: "Names, please."
OLE: Ole Johnson
LENA: Lena Johnson
CLERK: Any relations?
LENA (blushing): "Yah, vunce or tvice.
Ole couldn't vait."

What is it that's "Wet and Wild?"
A Norwegian with a stuck zipper.

. . . .

Did you hear about the Norwegian girl who had
a wooden baby?
Seems she got nailed by a carpenter.

. . . .

Ordinarily "TGIF" means "Thank goodness it's Friday."
Why do Norwegians have "TGIF" printed
on their shoes?
It means "Toes go in first."

. . . .

Ole took a notion to get into politics. He began making
speeches all over Minnesota, including the Indian reservations. He was giving a spirited address to members of
the Santee tribe and every time he made a stirring state-
ment, the tribal members would all shout: "OONGAH!
OONGAH!"
Ole felt he had made a good impression, so he stepped
off the platform so he could leave for his next stop. As one
of the Indians guided Ole to his car, he suddenly cautioned him:
"Watch out Ole . . . don't step in the Oongah."

TWO

Son of NORWEGIAN JOKES

How do you get a one-armed Norwegian
out of a tree?
—You wave at him.

. . . .

SWEDE: Ole, stand in front o my car and tell me
if my blinkers are working.
NORWEGIAN: yes . . . no . . . yes . . . no . . . yes
. . . no . . . yes . . . no . . . yes . . . no . . .

. . . .

Did you hear about the Norwegian who received a boo-
merang for his birthday? He went crazy trying to throw
away the old one.

LARS: Say Ole. I went by your house last night
and noticed you kissing your wife
in the window.
OLE: The yoke's on you. I vasn't even home
last night.

■ ■ ■ ■

The Norwegians in our community are so smart they have
finally figured out that they can also turn right on GREEN.

■ ■ ■ ■

Ole is teaching his Golden Labrador dog to jump out of an
airplane with a parachute. He calls him "Sky Lab."

■ ■ ■ ■

MAN: (Watching a funeral procession) "Who died?"
NORWEGIAN: I think it vas da guy in da casket.

■ ■ ■ ■

A Norwegian was driving his van with a huge aerial on it
for his CB radio. He turned a sharp corner whereupon the
aerial swivelled over toward the curb, spearing a lady
pedestrian. A few days later, infection set in. So she was
taken to the hospital where the doctor declared it the
worst case of van-aerial disease he'd ever seen.

LARS SAW OLE
KISSING HIS WIFE
IN THE WINDOW.

You don't believe Norwegians are athletic? My counsin, Ole, was the javelin catcher in the Olympics.

. . . .

Why did the Norwegian have the strong urge
to hit a laughing spiritualist?
Because he always liked to strike a happy
medium.

. . . .

Our dog got hold of some lutefisk the other day. He spent the next four days licking himself, trying to get rid of the taste.

. . . .

One day Ole went to work wearing one black shoe and one brown shoe. His co-worker, Sven, called his attention to it.
"Oh yah," said Ole. "I got anudder pair yust like it at home."

. . . .

The Doctor asked Ole when he discovered
he had diarrhea.
Said Ole, "Ven, I took off my bicycle clips."

At a cock fight, which one is the Norwegian?
—the one with the duck.
Which one is the Polack?
—The one that bets on the duck.
How do you know when the Mafia is involved?
—When the duck wins.

．．．．

A Norwegian visited his dentist for the fifth time in a month. Most of his teeth had been loosened and he had two black eyes. Said the dentist, "Out of curiosity, have you ever considered giving up married women?"

．．．．

Did you hear about the Norwegian who froze to death?
He was parked in front of a house of ill repute and was waiting for the red light to change.

．．．．

Ole comes from such a small town in Wisconsin . . . they have only one yellow page.
It's so small . . . McDonald's only has one arch.
And you have to order a Big Mac out of a catalogue.
They had to close the zoo . . . because the clam died.
And the local hooker is a virgin.

Ole says: Show me a country where all of the cars are rose colored . . . and I'll show you a pink car nation.

■   ■   ■   ■

A man approached a Norwegian minister about conducting a funeral service for his pet dog. The minister was indignant. "Why the very idea of asking an ordained minister of the gospel to preach a funeral for a dog!" The man shrugged and said, "Well, that's a shame you can't do it, because I figured on donating $10,000 to the church that would help me out."
"Well," exclaimed the minister. "Why didn't you tell me it was a LUTHERAN dog?"

■   ■   ■   ■

(Phone rings)
NORWEGIAN: "Sure is." (hangs up)
WIFE: "Who was it?"
NORWEGIAN: "I don't know. Some vun said,
"Long distance from New York. So I says, "Sure is."

■   ■   ■   ■

Did you hear about the Norwegian girl who was so thin that when she swallowed an olive, four guys left town?

46

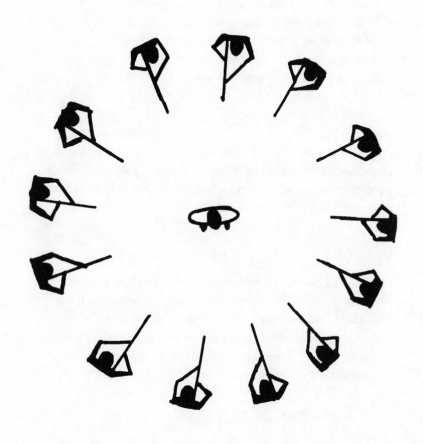

Norwegian Firing Squad

Thoughts from Ole: "Unless you're da lead dog . . .
da scenery never changes."
"If you're so smart, vhy aren't you rich?"
"Life is funny . . . ve must be built backvards . . .
my nose runs and my feet smell."

. . . .

A Norwegian woman stood on a street corner in the rain
with her dress over her head. A passerby expressed surprise, to which she responded, "Vell, dese legs are fifty
years old but dis hat is brand new."

. . . .

Hjalmar's cousin, Olav, came by bus to visit in Minneapolis. Olav called from a downtown phone booth to let
Hjalmar know he got in town OK. Hjalmar said, "Vell, vait
vhere you are and I'll come down and pick you up. Vhere
are you, Olav?" Olav glanced out of the phone booth and
answered, "I'm at the corner of Valk and Don't Valk."

. . . .

The Norwegian went back to Norway after his first trip to
the U.S.A. He was describing his experiences to friends:
"Vell, vhen I first got off the plane, I valked down the

street past a shurch, and dey va singing a song to me: "Ole, Ole, Ole." Den I vent to California and my cousin took me to Tijuana, Mexico, to see a bull fight. Dey musta recognized me dere, too, 'cause about every five minutes da crowd vould stand up and yell, "Ole' . . . Ole' . . . Ole'." But da strangest part about being in America is dat dose folks can't make up dere mind about anyting. You go to shurch and da folks all sing, "Stand up, Stand up for Yesus." Den you go to da ball game and everyone yells, "For Christ's sake, sit down."

．　．　．　．

A Norwegian was flying a helicopter when all of a sudden it came down to ground with a thud. Explained the Norwegian: "It vas getting cool up dere, so I turned off da fan."

．　．　．　．

Ole went from Duluth to Minneapolis one weekend. He met Hulda and they had a good time together. A few weeks later, Ole got a call from Hulda. Ole said, "How's tings vid you down in Minneapolis, Hulda?" "Dat's vat I'm calling you about, Ole," said Hulda. "I haven't been sick for two months." "Vell," exclaimed Ole, "Den you're lucky. Ve all haff had da flu up here in Duloot."

Ole helped a nun across the street during the rush hour. When they got across safely, the nun thanked Ole profusely. "Dat's OK," said Ole, "any friend of Zorro is a friend of mine."

■ ■ ■ ■

What's the happiest five years of a Norwegian's life?
—First grade.

■ ■ ■ ■

The Norse God, Thor, decided to go down to earth to be a mortal for an evening. He met a beautiful girl and they spent the evening together. In the morning, Thor thought he'd share his secret with the young lady, saying, "Honey, I'm Thor." "YOU'RE Thor???" she exclaimed. "Lithen, buthter, I'm tho thore I can hardly thit down."

■ ■ ■ ■

Ole, trying to explain the difference between Capitalism and Communism: "In Capitalism, Man exploits Man. Vid Communism, its da odder vay around."

■ ■ ■ ■

LENA: Do you have any trouble making up your mind?
TENA: Yes and no.

Lena got a phone call from her husband Lars announcing he had purchased a condominium. "Good," she told a neighbor lady. "Now I can throw away my diagram."

. . . .

There was a Norwegian who was so dumb he thought Abraham Lincoln was a Jewish automobile agency.

. . . .

Ole answered the phone and soon hung up the receiver. "Who vas it," inquired Lena. "Somevun must have thought dis vas the Coast Guard. All dey said vas, "Is da coast clear?"

. . . .

Know the toughest part about being a Norwegian in the summertime?
Driving around with the car windows rolled up so the neighbors will think you've got air conditioning.

. . . .

Why can't Norwegians trace their roots?
—Because Kunta Karlson dropped the family records overboard.

Norwegian Boat Builder

SVEN: Have you heard . . . dat dey elected a Pole to be Pope?
OLE: Yah, it's about time . . . dose Catlicks have had it long enough.

．　．　．　．

The Norwegian lady discovered that her husband, Bjarne, was fooling around. She called the undertaker, saying, "I vant you to come and pick up my husband's body." Inquired the undertaker, "When did he die?" She answered, "He starts tomorrow."

．　．　．　．

Ole came home to his apartment one night, snorting. "Dat Yanitor, vot a bragger. He claims he's made love to every voman in dis apartment except one."
"Hmmph" said Ole's wife. "Must be that snooty Mrs. Peterson on third floor."

．　．　．　．

Why hasn't there ever been a Norwegian president in the U.S.?
—Because they are expected to take a shower before inauguration.

A Norwegian plumber got a call from an apartment house owner instructing him to fix a leaky sink. But he cautioned the plumber to look out for a rather fierce dog in the apartment. "Just leave him be . . . don't try to pet him or be friendly. Just go fix the sink and it should be OK." The plumber did as instructed and found the growling dog, just as described. As he edged into the apartment, he heard a seductive voice from the bedroom, "Come on right in, honey." Emboldened, the Norwegian headed toward the bedroom, keeping an eye on the menacing dog. Once more he heard, "Come on right in, honey." He excitedly turned the corner into the bedroom and guess what he found? A parrot in the cage! Chagrined, he decided to just fix the leaky sink and leave. After making the repair, he prepared to leave, still keeping an eye on the growling dog. As he passed the parrot's cage, he muttered, "Is that all you can say, you stupid parrot: 'Come right on in, honey'?" "No . . ." said the parrot . . . "I can say SIC 'EM!"

. . . .

Tina was being interviewed for a job as maid for the snooty Mrs. Vander Rocks, who inquired: "Do you have any religious views?"
"No," said Tina, but I've got some nice pictures of Norvay."

A Norwegian decided to raise chickens so he planted 500 of them completely under the soil. Of course, they all died. So he ordered 500 more and planted them with the heads sticking out. Still they all died. So the Norwegian sat down and wrote a letter to the University of Oslo, describing the situation. A few weeks later, he got a reply: "Please send soil sample."

■ ■ ■ ■

ENGLISHMAN: Yes . . . we have only the finest furniture here in our castle. For example, that beautiful hand made bed goes back to Louis the Fourteenth.
NORWEGIAN: Vell, I'm in about da same boat. If ve don't make a payment, our furniture goes back
to Sears the Fifteenth.

■ ■ ■ ■

A Norwegian was consulted to help a Japanese firm name their new compact car. The Norwegian asked how soon they would require the name; he was advised it was needed within two weeks.
"Dot soon?" he asked.
The Japanese misunderstood and thought that was the name he had chosen . . . so they put their own spelling on the car . . . the Datsun.

A Norwegian, about to get married, asked his cousin what he should do on the wedding night. The cousin, a bit too reserved to be explicit, merely advised, "After you get your clothes off, just rub her stomach and say, 'I love you, I love you.' The rest will come natural." So, after the wedding, the couple retired to their room where they disrobed. The Norwegian remembered the instructions, so he rubbed his new bride's stomach, saying "I love you, I love you." "Lower . . . Lower . . . ," said the bride excitedly. So the Norwegian spoke again but in a much deeper bass voice, "I LOVE YOU, I LOVE YOU."

■   ■   ■   ■

A Norwegian made a boo boo in traffic and dented the fender on another car. The driver of that car pulled the Norwegian out of his car and after chalking a circle on the pavement, instructed the Norwegian to stand in that circle and not move. Then the angered motorist proceeded to bash in the Norwegian's car . . . smashing the headlights, ramming in the fender, etc. As he glanced around, he noticed the Norwegian gleefully laughing as he watched the scene. This angered the motorist even more, so he demanded to know why the Norwegian was laughing and smiling as he watched his car being demolished. The Norwegian explained, "Vell, vehen you vasn't vatching . . . I stepped out of dat circle six times."

The space program sent a monkey and a Norwegian on a space flight. The monkey's job was to perform certain scientific routines, pushing levers, etc. The Norwegian's job was to feed the monkey.

∎ ∎ ∎ ∎

A Norwegian noticed his car being stolen, so he chased it down the street trying to copy down the license number.

∎ ∎ ∎ ∎

KNUTE: Dis grizzly bear is vun I got vid my club.
TENA: How brave of you. How big a club?
KNUTE: 50 guys. It vas my Sons of Norvay club.

∎ ∎ ∎ ∎

Norwegian doctors have quit circumcising Norwegians. They have found they were throwing away the best part.

A Norwegian who had been drinking heavily got on an elevator. At the next floor he was surprised to see a naked woman get on. He took a long look at the unusual sight and remarked, "Shay . . . you know, my vife has got an outfit yust like dat."

■ ■ ■ ■

The Norwegian woman was dying, and in her final hours she sympathetically wished her husband a happy life when she was gone. "In fact, Lars," she said, "when I am gone, I tink you should get yourself anudder vife. And you can even give her my dresses." "Von't vork," answered Lars, "She's a 9 and you're an 18."

■ ■ ■ ■

Know how a Norwegian lost 5 pounds?
He took a bath.

■ ■ ■ ■

ARNE: My brother says he's sick.
DOCTOR: Now, Arne, you're brother's hale and hearty. He just THINKS he's sick.

Two days later.
DOCTOR: How's your brother?
ARNE: He thinks he's dead.

Why did the Norwegian wear two jackets while painting? Because the directions on the paint can said, "Put on two coats."

. . . .

What do Eric the Red and Smokey the Bear have in common?
—They both have the same middle name.

. . . .

BERTHA: Is Lena a good housekeeper?
TINA: I should say she is . . . she's been married three times and kept the house every time.

. . . .

Three ministers formed a friendship and met each week for coffee to discuss their mutual vocation. They finally got on such good terms they decided one day to confess their sinful weaknesses to each other, figuring such openness would be good for their psychological well being. The first minister confessed to an occasional binge on cigarettes and bourbon . . . then back to the straight life for a few weeks until the urge hit him again. The second minister, a rather dapper fellow, owned up to a weakness for women. "I just can't help myself," he said, "so every two months or so I find a woman to satisfy my lusts. It is a terrible weakness, but I just can't seem to help it." The third minister, a Norwegian and probably of the Lutheran faith, took his turn in the confessional trio. "Vell," he began. "I have vun very terrible sin. And dat is, I love to gossip. And I yust can't vait to get out of here."

. . . .

LENA: I yust bought myself a new hat. I like to buy a hat for myself ven I'm down in the dumps.
OLE: Hmmm . . . I vundered vere you found it.

. . . .

A Norwegian, a German and an Englishman were sentenced to death in Iran. The firing squad aimed their rifles at the German who was asked if he had any last words. He suddenly shouted at the top of his lungs . . . "TORNADO!" Everyone scattered. When order was resumed, they found the German had escaped. So they lined up the Englishman and asked if he had any last words. "Earthquake! Earthquake" he screamed. Everyone dove for safety and the Englishman escaped in the melee. After they restored order, they brought the Norwegian in front of the firing squad and asked if he had any final words. Yelled the Norwegian: "FIRE!!!" So they did.

Two Norwegians were hunting ducks. At the end of the day, they'd had no luck. Ole turned to Lars and asked, "Do you tink ve maybe haven't been trowing the dog high enough?"

■   ■   ■   ■

Lena doesn't worry about Ole chasing women. She says, "Da dog chases cars, but he don't know how to drive."

■   ■   ■   ■

OLGA: You remember my uncle Kristoffer . . . ven he came to dis country, he didn't have a pot to do it in.
TENA: Vat is he doing now, den?
OLGA: Selling pots.

■   ■   ■   ■

Ole met his friend Alfred one day in downtown Fargo. Ole told about all the problems he'd been having. His wife had run off with the preacher. His son was on drugs. His daughter was leading a life of sin. And he'd had several lawsuits filed on him. Alfred responded sympathetically. "Sorry to hear about dat, Ole. By da vay, vat are you doing dese days?" "Same ting," said Ole, "selling good luck charms."

Norway recently negotiated with Sweden for the purchase of snow to use as land-fill.

■   ■   ■   ■

NORWEGIAN: How much are your eggs?
GROCER: 90 cents a dozen, whole, and 40 cents for cracked.
NORWEGIAN: Vell, how about cracking me a dozen?

■   ■   ■   ■

We once met a Norwegian named "Sam Ting." We asked how he got the name. "Vell, ven I came to dis country, da guy ahead of me told da immigration man dat his name vas Ole Olson. I vas next and dey asked my name, and I said, "Sam Ting." So, I been Sam Ting ever since.

■   ■   ■   ■

Ole and Lena's Sons of Norway chapter had a guest speaker who was a science professor at St. Olaf College in Northfield, Minn. The professor told of advances in science that would enable an apartment owner to heat an entire apartment building for a whole year with just one lump of coal. Ole turned to Lena and snorted, "Who's he kidding? Our landlord has been doing dat for years."

THIS IS A NORWEGIAN DUCK CALL

THIS IS A NORWEGIAN
USING A NORWEGIAN
DUCK CALL

Lena is so fat that when she decided to take up jogging, they made her take the truck route.

■ ■ ■ ■

A Norwegian strolled into the Grand Hotel in Oslo and asked for a room.
Clerk: Sorry . . . no more rooms available.
Norwegian: If King Olav came in, would you have a room for him?
Clerk: Why, certainly.
Norwegian: "Vell, he ain't coming, so give me his room."

■ ■ ■ ■

LENA: What ever happened to our sex relations?
OLE: As I recall, ve didn't even get a Christmas card from dem.

■ ■ ■ ■

There's a fellow in our town . . . a Norwegian . . . who is really ugly. When he was born, the doctor slapped his mother. His mother was so ashamed of him, she borrowed another baby for the baptism. His parents had to tie a pork chop around his neck to get his dog to play with him. One night a woman stopped him on the street and asked him to follow her to her home. There, she asked him into the bedroom. Anticipating some excitement, he followed. In the bed was a little boy sniffing and crying. "There," said the woman. "I told you, Junior, if you didn't stop crying and go to sleep, I'd bring the boogy man in!"

■　■　■　■

Uncle Torvald is getting to the age where his only reason for wanting to get on the Love Boat is to play shuffle board.

■　■　■　■

Cousin Hjalmar's wife just presented him with their fifth child, which Hjalmar promptly named "Chang."
His explanation: "I read in the paper that every fifth child born is Chinese."

■　■　■　■

We heard recently that a Norwegian broke his shoulder during a pie eating contest. A cow fell on him.

■　■　■　■

JOHAN: Vell, now dat I've turned 65, from now on our love making vill have to be infrequent.
INGEBORG: Is dat vun vord or two?

Why don't Norwegians swat flies?
It's their national bird.

■   ■   ■   ■

The highway patrolman stopped the Norwegian's car and informed the Norwegian that his wife had fallen out of the car three miles back. "Thank goodness," exclaimed the Norwegian. "I thought I'd gone deaf."

■   ■   ■   ■

The Norwegian got a job in the fertilizer factory. The boss tried to determine the extent of the Norwegian's abilities. "Tell me, do you know anything about Nitrates?" Answered the Norwegian . . . "All I know is dey are cheaper dan day rates."

If you see a Norwegian walking around with bleeding wounds on his face . . . don't worry. It's just another Norsky who's been trying to learn to eat with a fork.

■ ■ ■ ■

There's a town near Mt. Horeb, Wisconsin where they kept the old fire engine when they bought a new one even though the motor was shot in the old engine. When asked why, the Chief answered, "Ve're saving dat vun for false alarms."

■ ■ ■ ■

A Norwegian was hitchhiking and was given a ride in a pickup truck by two Swedes. While the Norwegian was riding in the back of the pickup, the Swedes accidentally drove into the river. The Norwegian drowned because he couldn't get the tailgate open.

■ ■ ■ ■

TORVALD: Everybody should believe in something.
OLE: "Vell, I believe I'll have a drink."

■ ■ ■ ■

A Norwegian received cuff links and a short sleeved shirt for his birthday. So he had his wrists pierced.

67

A Norwegian was taking a chicken home for egg laying and eventual Sunday dinner. On the way, he thought he'd take in a movie he'd wanted to see. So he tucked the chicken down into his trousers so the management wouldn't know. He sat down next to two women. During the show, the chicken got restless and stuck its head out of the Norwegian's trousers. One of the gals spied the sight in the darkened theater, and leaned over to report that the Norwegian was exposing himself. "Why Mable, haven't you ever seen one before?" giggled Gertie. "Yes, I certainly have, but this is the first one that ever tried to eat the popcorn out of my sack."

■ ■ ■ ■

DANE: Is that Hortense over by the bar?
NORWEGIAN: She looks pretty relaxed to me.

■ ■ ■ ■

Ole and Lena, while in the drug store, spied a display of Milk of Magnesia, which proclaimed in the poster, "Makes you feel youthful." Ole thought he would like to feel younger, so he bought a bottle and immediately drank it down. As they strolled down the road toward home, Lena asked him every few minutes whether he felt youthful as yet. After about a mile and a half, she asked him again: "Ole, do you feel youthful now?" "Vell," said Ole, "I don't know dat I feel so yout'ful . . . but I just did something awful childish."

Ole recently won the famous NORWEGIAN MILLION DOLLAR LOTTERY. He gets a dollar a year for a million years.

■ ■ ■ ■

Did you hear about the Norwegian burglar who broke into the Elks Club?
He was apprehended because he signed the guest book on the way out.

■ ■ ■ ■

How do Norwegians refer to milk?
—They call it the "Udder Cola"

■ ■ ■ ■

Lena lay dying, and on her deathbed she decided to make a confession. "Ole, I have to confess to you before I go dat I vas unfaithful to you."
'Dat's OK, Lena," answered Ole. "I have a confession to make, too. It vas me dat poisoned you."

■ ■ ■ ■

INSURANCE SALESMAN: Now before we complete this policy, do you want an Ordinary Life?
NORWEGIAN: "Vell, I VOULD like to fool around a little on Saturday night."

During a Christmas program, the Norwegian kept singing the words . . . LEON . . . LEON . . . LEON. The person standing next to him whispered in his ear that he was holding the song book upside down.

. . . .

Ole has a 4-60 model air conditioner in his car. Four windows open, 60 miles an hour.

. . . .

A Norwegian, attending a play, decided to leave after the first act. He explained, "Vell it says on da program, 'Act 2, nine months later.' I don't have time to vait, so I better get going."

. . . .

Some Norwegians were playing a bunch of Swedes in a game of football. When the six o'clock whistle blew, the Swedes went home. Four plays later, the Norwegians scored a touchdown.

. . . .

SVEN: How's your brudder doing at dat salesman yob?
OLE: Vell, he got two orders yesterday. Get out . . . and Stay out.

Norwegian Garbage Disposal

A Norwegian was trying to find out how to insure that he would pass the test to become a citizen of the U.S. He talked to an Irishman who assured him that it was easy if he could answer the questions. The Irishman confided that he gained citizenship by the simple method of writing the answers inside his shorts, then sneaking a peek downward during the exam. The Norwegian thought this was a marvelous idea, so he paid the Irishman $5 to loan him the shorts. Only the Norwegian didn't notice he put them on backward. During the citizenship examination he was first asked, "Who is President of the United States?" The Norwegian glanced downward and answered, "J.C. Penney." Next question: "How many states in the Union?" The Norwegian again furtively glanced down, and answered confidently, "30½." Then the final question: "What colors in the American Flag?" Once more the Norwegian sneaked a peek, and came up with his answer: "Brown and White."

A collector of rare books heard that Ole had an old family Bible that had been in his family for generations. Upon visiting Ole, the collector learned that Ole had thrown the Bible away. Ole explained it was very old and was printed by someone named "Guten-something or other." "Not Gutenberg?" gasped the collector. "Yah, dat vas da name," said Ole. "You idiot! You threw away one of the first books ever printed. A copy recently sold at auction for $500,000." "Vell," said Ole, "mine vouldn't haff been vorth a nickel. Some guy by da name of Martin Luther had scribbled all over it."

. . . .

Ole and Lena were expecting their first baby. As the time approached, Lena announced, "I tink it's time for da baby . . . but vid da traffic dis time of day, I'm not sure ve vill get to da hospital in time."
Ole thought a minute and then said, "Vell, maybe ve better take two cars. Dat vay, vun of us is sure to make it."

. . . .

An elderly Swede of about 78 years went to a local house of ill repute.
Swede: How much do you charge?
Madam: Fifty dollars.
Swede: You're putting me on!
Madam: OK, but that's $10 extra.

The Norwegian showed up for work with bandaged ears. "What happened," asked a fellow worker. "Vell," said the Norwegian. "Last night I was ironing my shirt vhen da phone rang and I picked up da iron by mistake." "Well, what happened to the other ear," asked the companion. "Oh . . . dat. Vell, I had to call da doctor."

■ ■ ■ ■

Sven says: "Dere is two signs of old age. Vun is losing your memory . . . and . . . I forget da udder vun."

■ ■ ■ ■

A Norwegian who was an electrician in the Navy was discharged following his term of duty. His first job as a civilian was to do the wiring at an Oklahoma Indian reservation, his particular job being the wiring for the bathroom facilities. This Norwegian will go down in history as being the first person to wire a head for a reservation.

■ ■ ■ ■

KNUTE: Ole, vhy don't you play golf vid Emil anymore?
OLE: Vould you play golf vid a guy who doesn't count all his strokes, and kicks da ball out of da rough vid his foot?
KNUTE: No, I certainly vouldn't.
OLE: Vell, needer vould Emil.

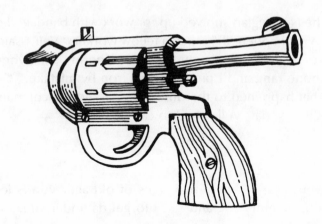

Norwegian Pistol

Why does it take 15 Norwegians to milk a cow?
—Four to hang on to the faucets, and 11 to move
the cow up and down.

■ ■ ■ ■ ■

A Norwegian joined a chain letter club. At last report, he
has received 579 chains.

■ ■ ■ ■

Maybe you heard about the Norwegian who fell into a
lens grinding machine and made a spectacle of himself.

A Norwegian in our town flunked his drivers test. He opened the car door to let out the clutch.

■ ■ ■ ■

PERSONNEL DIRECTOR: Before I consider you for a job, do you lie, cheat, steal or come in late?
NORWEGIAN: No . . . I never have.
But I'm villing to learn.

■ ■ ■ ■

Ole says that Lena is a fast talker . . . 300 words per minute . . . with gusts to 500.

■ ■ ■ ■

PASTOR: You claim you can't donate because you owe everyone. Don't you feel you owe the Lord something?
NORWEGIAN: "Yes, but He isn't pushing me like da rest of dem are."

■ ■ ■ ■

A Norwegian set out to swim the English Channel. But half way across he got tired and swam back.

Why does it take 3 Norwegians to replace
a light bulb?
One to hold the bulb and two to turn the ladder.

• • • •

TORKEL: My vife is alvays asking for money. Last
veek she asked for $100.
Yesterday she asked me for $200.
And today she vanted $300.
TRVGVE: Vat in da vorld does she do vid it all?
TORKEL: I don't know. I never give her any.

• • • •

Lars wasn't too smart; but he managed to make a fine living buying and selling used cars. He'd buy a car for $100
and sell it for $400, for example. Lars explained, "I ain't
too good at figures, but I'm satisfied vid a 3% profit."

• • • •

Ole showed up for work with two black eyes. Someone
asked him what happened so he told about going to the
ballgame the night before. A lady stood up in front of him
during an exciting play in the game, and Ole had noticed
her dress tucked in the "cheeks" of her seat. "So," Ole

said, "I decided to be a yentleman and pull out da dress. And dat's ven she hauled off and slugged me in da eye." "So, how'd you get the other black eye," inquired his crony. "Vell," said Ole, "ven I saw how mad she was, I tucked it back in."

▪ ▪ ▪ ▪

A Norwegian inherited an exotic animal called a "Rary." At first, he enjoyed the novelty of owning such an unusual pet; but he soon noticed the animal was eating and growing like mad. Eventually the animal grew to the point that the Norwegian knew he had to get rid of it. So he loaded it into a freight car and took it all the way from Wisconsin to the Grand Canyon in Arizona. There, he led the Rary to the edge of the Canyon. As the Norwegian's cousin, Ole, looked on, the Norwegian tipped the Rary over the rim of the canyon. Whereupon Ole was heard to remark, "Dat's a long, long vay to tip a Rary."

▪ ▪ ▪ ▪

The Norwegian got into a bad fight and killed a man. Lena came to see him in prison and asked what sentence had been passed. Said Ole: "Dey sentenced me to be electrocuted." Answered Lena: "don't vorry, Ole. I'll vait for you."

Ole decided to divorce Lena. His friend, Lars, expressed surprise. "Why are you divorcing Lena after all she's been through with you?" asked Lars.

"Why you went through the drouth when the grasshoppers got all of the crops that didn't burn up. Then you got a job in town and when you lost it, Lena went to work. And when you got another job and broke your hip in an accident, Lena was right there with you. And when you got in that legal trouble, why Lena stuck right with you. After all that, WHY, Ole would you divorce Lena?"

Ole thought a moment, and then remarked, "Vell, I got to figuring she must be a jinx."

■ ■ ■ ■

The Olson family built a fancy new house in town and they were anxious to show it off to their friends. So they sent out invitations for a party. On the party night, Mrs. Olson suddenly remembered they didn't have any toilet paper for their fancy indoor bathroom. So she sent Mr. Olson out to buy some. But no stores were open. So they settled on cutting up some of Mrs. Olson's old dress patterns which were of tissue paper. The party was a success and afterward, two of the Norwegian ladies were discussing how fancy everything was. "Yah," said Mrs. Thorson, "dey are so fancy dat dey got special toilet paper, some marked "Front" and some marked "Back."

TINA: Have you been to see Dr. Zhivago?
LENA: No . . . ve alvays go to Dr. Gittelson.

■　■　■　■

Ole the Norwegian loved his wife, Lena . . . even though she was a bad cook and left the food on the burner too long. When she finally presented Ole with a new baby, everyone in town held their breath when it was learned the baby had a rather dusky skin. But that didn't bother Ole. He just smiled and said, "Yah, dat Lena . . . she just burns everything."

■　■　■　■

Two Norwegians were sent up in a space capsule. During the flight, one of them went on a scheduled space walk outside the capsule. During the space walk, the door accidentally closed. So the Norwegian inside the capsule suddenly heard a rapping on the door. "Yah, who iss it?" he inquired.

■　■　■　■

Did you hear about the man who was half Norwegian and half Japanese? Every December 7th, he goes out and attacks Pearl Olson.

THE PHILOSOPHY OF OLE

"Vifes are like baseball umpires; dey never believe a
man is safe ven he's out."

"If you vant to soar vid da eagles in da morning
You can't hoot vid da owls at night."

"If you tink your yobs are small
And da revards are few
Yust remember dat da mighty oak
Vas vunce a nut like yew."

"I always eat my peas vid honey
I've dun it all my life
It may seem kinda funny
But it keeps dem on my knife."

"Dere's vun kind of a liar a man can tolerate.
Dat's a good looking blonde who tells him he's
looking younger every day."

■ ■ ■ ■

A Norwegian came out of a hotel rather inebriated. He
spotted a tall man in a blue uniform with gold braid so he
approached him and said, "Say, Mister, call me a taxi."
The uniformed man stiffened and said coldly, "My good
man, I am an Admiral." "Vell," said the drunk . . . "den
call me a boat."

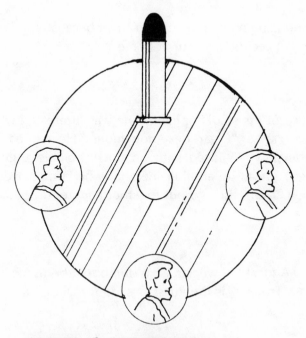

HOW TO MAKE A
NORWEGIAN QUARTER

MATERIALS: ONE LARGE WASHER
• 3 PENNIES
• 1 22 CALIBER SHELL
  (22 + 3 = 25)
EPOXY SHELL AND PENNIES TO WASHER

Ole and Lena moved to another town because they read that most accidents occur at home.

. . . .

Because of his smoking habit, Ole was interested when he heard about "Cigarettes Anonymous." He learned that members, when faced with an uncontrolable urge to smoke . . . call up another member who comes over to see you. Then, they go out together and get drunk.

. . . .

A local Norwegian is so dumb that he thinks "Trotsky" is the Russian word for Diarrhea.

. . . .

OLE: What do dey call dat kind of bed dat has a kind of tent over it?
LARS: Canopy?
OLE: No . . . dat's UNDER da bed.

. . . .

Ole remembers the depression times vividly. "I can remember," he tells little Ole, "dat ven I stepped on a dime, my shoe soles vere so thin I could tell vhedder it vas heads or tails."

Then we heard about the Norwegian who cut down a big grove of trees with a chain saw. When he got through, someone showed him how to start the engine.

. . . .

SWIMMER: "Are there any sharks in these waters?"
OLE: Not any more.
SWIMMER: What happened to them?
OLE: The Piranhas got 'em.

. . . .

JUDGE: Mr. Olson, I'm going to give you 50 dollars or 10 days.
OLE: Vell, I'm short of money, so I'll take da 50 dollars.

. . . .

LARS: Vat do you call it ven you get bit by a bee right after a mosquito?
HELMER: "Sting along vid itch."

The fire department got a fire call, and it was from the Norwegian farmer.

"How do we get out to your place, Ole?",
inquired the fire chief.

"Vell," said Ole, "You might use dat little red truck you got dere at da fire station."

•   •   •   •

How can it be proved that Adam was a Norwegian?
Who else would stand beside a naked woman and just eat an apple?

•   •   •   •

ARNIE: If it took nine men 9 hours to build a brick wall, how much time would it take 6 men to build it?
RALPH: None...because the nine men have already done the work.

•   •   •   •

When Ole and Lena got married and went on their honeymoon, Lena was a bit bashful. As they walked up to the hotel, Lena said, "Vhat can ve do so dey von't know ve're newlyveds?"

   Answered Ole: "YOU carry da luggage."

A Cannibal was checking out prices at his local meat market. He asked the vendor why the Irishman cost 90 cents a pound, the German 85 cents a pound and the Norwegian was priced $1.50 per pound.

"Why does the Norwegian cost so much?" he asked.

"Well," came the answer, "did you ever try to clean one?"

■   ■   ■   ■

A plane carrying Jimmy Carter, Gerald Ford, Henry Kissinger, a Priest, and a Norwegian hippy was crossing the U.S. when it developed engine trouble. The pilot and co-pilot had parachutes and baled out, informing the others that there were four parachutes left. Seeing that here were five persons left abroad, Jimmy Carter said, "The American people would want their president saved." So, he grabbed one of the parachutes and jumped. Gerald Ford declared that as Ex-President, he should also be saved, so he grabbed a parachute, and out the hatch he went. Henry Kissinger then said, "Since I am da schmartest man in da world, I should be saved," so he grabbed a pack and leaped out of the plane. The Priest said, "Well, with only one parachute left, I have decided to stay on the plane. I have had a good life and am at peace with my maker. So I will remain." "Von't be necessary," said the Norwegian hippy. "Da smartest man in the vorld yust yumped out vid my back pack."

Ole took his wife to the doctor who gave her a physical. He took Ole aside and said, "There's really nothing seriously wrong with your wife. I'd say everything would be OK if she had sex 7 or 8 times a month." "Vell," said Ole, "dat sounds fine. You could put me down for a couple times."

.   .   .   .

Ole was talking to Lars about the problems of growing old. Said Ole, "I heard da odder day dat dere is FOUR stages of getting older.
Stage One . . . is forgetting FACES.
Stage Two . . . is forgetting NAMES
Stage Three . . . is forgetting to zip UP.
"Yah," said Lars. "Vhat is da fourth stage?"
Ole: Forgetting to zip DOWN!

.   .   .   .

Ole did some carpenter work for a mental asylum and one day he noticed his car had a flat tire. While trying to change the tire, Ole lost 5 studs in the mud. One of the inmates walked up and suggested that Ole take one stud off each wheel and that would last until he got to the garage. Ole was amazed and said, "That is good thinking. By the way, why are you in here?"
Inmate: For being crazy, not STUPID.

Sven asked Ole for advice on how to get himself duded up to go out with his new girl friend, Helga. Ole recommened that Sven get cleaned up a bit, and then douse himself with toilet water. Sven tried it out, but had the misfortune of having the lid fall on him.

■ ■ ■ ■

A Norwegian grocery boy was filling a lady's grocery sack. "I'll yust put da eggs on da bottom of da sack, lady," he said. "Dat vay, if da eggs break, dey von't mess up da canned goods.

■ ■ ■ ■

A Norwegian insurance salesman took the afternoon off and went to a triple-X movie. In his daily sales report he wrote, "Went to see a couple who weren't covered."

■ ■ ■ ■

Two nuns were driving by the unemployment office in LaCrosse, Wisconsin when their car had a tire blow out. One of the men in the unemployment line offered to fix the tire if the nuns would keep his place in line. As Ole drove by with Lars and witnessed the scene, he remarked, "Tings must be tough all over nowdays . . . even da Pope is laying dem off."

THREE

Grandson of NORWEGIAN JOKES

Tina applied for a job in an office. In hiring her, the boss explained, "In six months, you will be eligible for a raise, provided you work diligently."

Tina muttered under her breath, "I knew dere was a catch to it."

■ ■ ■ ■

Ole and Lena had nine very handsome children. Then came a tenth child . . . but this one . . . to be blunt . . . was extremely ugly. Ole thought about it for some time, then one day, he confronted Lena. "Lena . . . tell me da truth . . . is dat last youngster really mine?"

"Yah, Ole," confessed Lena. "Dat last baby is yours. But da others AREN'T."

Ole's son Hjalmar didn't graduate from the top half of his class . . . but he had the distinction of being in the half that made the TOP half possible.

■　■　■　■

Some one asked Lars if he knew who the greatest inventors were.
"Sure," said Lars, "Dere vas dat Irish guy, Pat Pending; and da Russian guy, U.S. Regpatoff."

■　■　■　■

SVEN: Olson got a bicycle for his wife.
TRYG: How in da vorld did he get such a lucky trade?

■　■　■　■

Philosophy of Ole: "Money don't buy happiness . . . but needer does poverty."

■　■　■　■

As Ole lay dying, he asked his wife: "Lena, vould you get me some of dat lutefisk you got cooking on da stove?"
"I'm sorry," said Lena, "I'm saving dat for after da funeral."

A DOG NAMED SEX
(Written by a Norwegian)

For protection, my grandfather got me a German Shepherd dog. Ven he found out I vas Norvegian, da dog bit me. He vas a vonderful vatch dog. Vun night vhile I vas being held up by a robber, da dog vatched.

Most people who have dogs call dem Rover or Spot. I called my dog "Sex." As I later found out, Sex is an embarrassing name. Last veek I took Sex for a valk and he ran away from me. I spent hours looking for da dog. A cop came over and asked me, "What are you doing in the alley at 4 in the morning?" I replied, "Looking for Sex." My case comes up Thursday.

Vun day I vent to City Hall to get a dog license, and told the clerk, "I vould like a license for Sex." He said, "I would like one too." So, I said, "But dis is a dog." And he said, "I don't care how she looks." So I said, "You don't understand; I've had Sex since I vas two years old." He said, "You must have been a very strong baby."

I told him dat vehn my vife and I separated, ve vent to court to fight for custody of da dog. I said, "Your Honor, I had Sex before I vas married." And he said, "Me too."

Den I told him dat after I got married, Sex left me; he said, "Me too." Vhen I told him dat vun time I had Sex on TV, he said, "Show off!" I told him it vas a contest. He said, "You should have sold tickets."

I also told da judge about da time vhen my vife and I vere on our honeymoon and ve took along da dog. I told da clerk dat I vanted a room to sleep in and anodder room for Sex. Da clerk said dat every room in da motel vas for Sex.

Den, I said, "You don't understand. Sex keeps me avake at night." And da clerk said, "Me too."

I give up!

■ ■ ■ ■

OLE: Tell me, Doctor. How do I stand?
DOCTOR: That's what puzzles me, Ole.

■ ■ ■ ■

They were planning to put up a statute of Uncle Torvald over in Norway. But they ran out of Silly Putty.

■ ■ ■ ■

OLE: Torvald, what do you tink about LSD?
TORVALD: Vell, he vas a pretty decent President.
OLE: No . . . I mean da dope.
TORVALD: Oh, him. Vell, dey kicked him out of office, so I suppose ve're all done vid him.
OLE: What do you tink about da farm bill?
TORVALD: Vell, if ve owe it, I s'pose ve should pay it.

Dear Olaf:

I'm not sure you vill be interested in dis, but it could make you a lot of money vid a small investment of only $50,000. Since you own dat fleet of herring boats, I figure you got enough money to sving it.

I am inviting yust a few good friends to inwest vid me in a large Cat ranch near Oslo, Norway. We vould start vid about a million cats. Each cat averages about 20 cents for the white ones and up to 40 cents for the black. Dis vill give us 12 million cat skins per year to sell for an average of about 32 cents, making our gross revenue about 4 million dollars a year. Dis averages out to be about $11,000 a day, including Sundays and holidays.

A good Norwegian Cat man can skin about 50 cats, working part time each day for $3.15. It vill take 663 men to operate da ranch, so da net profit vould be over $9,200 per day. Our $50,000 investment vould be recovered in 5.3 days.

Da cats vould be fed on rats exclusively. Rats multiply four times as fast as cats. Ve vould start a Rat ranch adjacent to our cat farm. If ve start vid a million rats, ve vill have four rats per cat per day. Da rats will be fed on da carcasses of da cats dat ve skin. Dis vill give each rat a quarter of a cat. You can see da business is clean, self-supporting, and automatic. Da cats will eat da rats and da rats will eat da cats and ve vill get da skins.

Ewentually, I hope to cross da cats vid snakes so dey vill

skin demselves tvice a year. Dis vould save da labor cost of skinning as vell as give us two skins for each cat.

Let me know if you are interested, Olaf. I am radder choosey about who gets into dis skinning operation. I am reserving a wery attractive engraved certificate dat I vill send you upon receipt of your cash for vhatever share of da operation you vant to own.

Remember, cash only. No checks!
Your good buddy,

Knute

■ ■ ■ ■

Lars met Ole on the main street one day. Ole had a disgusted look on his face as he exclaimed, PTOOIE! WHAT A DRIVER.
"What's boddering you, Ole?" asked Lars.
"Vell," said Ole, "I vas vatching a lady try to park her great big car in a little parking space . . . and I said to her, 'Lady, if you can park dat big car in dat little space, I'll kiss your behind.' PTOOIE! WHAT A DRIVER!"

■ ■ ■ ■

Ole bought Lena a wig because he heard she was "getting bald" at the office.

There was the Norwegian so dumb he thought a polaroid was a condition that came from sitting on the ice.

■ ■ ■ ■

Another Norwegian gave his mother-in-law a cemetery plot for her birthday. Next year he gave her nothing. When his wife asked why not, the Norwegian answered, "Vell, she didn't use da present I gave her last year."

■ ■ ■ ■

Ole ran into his old buddy, Hjalmar, and asked how his divorce was coming. "Not so good," sighed Hjalmar. "My vife von't give me a divorce until she can figure out a vay to do it vidout making me happy."

95

Ole reports he recently had a nightmare . . . his wife and Dolly Parton were fighting over him. And his wife won.

. . . .

Uncle Torvald was lecturing little Lars
on his bad manners.
"Lars . . . you are eating like a little pig.
You know what a little pig is, don't you?"
"Yah," said little Lars. "A little pig
is a hog's little boy."

. . . .

A Norwegian had to bail out of an airplane. He pulled the first ripcord, but nothing happened. So he pulled the emergency ripcord . . . and again, nothing happened. Bewildered, he looked around as he rapidly approached the ground. To his amazement, he saw another man . . . ascending upward at a rapid rate. "Hey . . ." yelled the Norwegian . . . "what do you know about parachutes?" "Not much," called back the other man . . . "I happen to specialize in gas stoves."

. . . .

Ole says that Lena is on a banana diet. "She hasn't lost any weight," reports Ole . . . "but you should see her climb trees."

A Norwegian airline pilot complained that the runway in Minneapolis was only 100 feet long. "I can't see why dey made it so short . . . ven dey made it tree miles vide."

■　■　■　■

Have you seen the Norwegian Toronado?
It's a '54 Chevy with snow tires on the front.

■　■　■　■

OLE: Say Torvald . . . you're hair is getting kinda thin on top. Don't you think you maybe ought get a toupee?
TORVALD: Heck no . . . I don't see no sense in getting a new top for a convertible . . . when da motor's shot.

■　■　■　■

A Pole kidnapped a Norwegian kid . . . so he sent him home with a ransom note. The kid's parents sent him back with the money.

■　■　■　■

At the Sons of Norway annual meeting, the treasurer reported a deficit of $100. One of the Norwegians stood up and said, "I vote we donate half of it to the Red Cross and the other 75 to the Salvation Army."

Success Story: Ole says, "When I came to dis country, I didn't have a nickel. Now . . . I have a nickel."

. . . .

Ole and Lena had been married 12 years with no off-spring. One day Lena announced that Ole was going to become a papa. Uff Da! Ole vas so overjoyed . . . in fact, he exclaimed that he was going down to the paper to put in a notice so their friends would know the good news. When he got back home, Lena asked, "Did you put da notice in da paper, Ole?" "Yah I did," said Ole. "How much did it cost?" asked Lena. "$900," answered Ole. "Uff da!" exclaimed Lena. "Dat's an awful lot. Vot did dey tell you?" "Vell," said Ole, "Da lady asked me 'how many insertions?' So, I said three times a week for twelve years."

. . . .

Ole invited some friends over to his house for a Saturday night party. He took Torvald aside for specific instructions on how to get there, adding, "Go to da fifth floor and when you see Apartment D, push da doorbell button vid your elbow, and ven da door opens, put your foot against it and valk in." "Vat in the vorld vould I go tru all dat rig-amarole for, Ole?" asked the puzzled Torvald. "Vell," said Ole, "you vouldn't vant to come empty handed, vould you?"

LENA: Vhy do you go on da balcony vhen I sing? Don't you like to hear me sing?

OLE: Vell, I yust vant da neighbors to see I'm not beating my vife.

■ ■ ■ ■

OLE: Did you hear about the Norwegian who married a Mexican woman and they had twins?

LARS: No. What did they name them?

OLE: José and Hose B.

■ ■ ■ ■

A Norwegian found a bottle on the street, rubbed it a bit to dust it off…suddenly a genie popped out, thanked the Norwegian, and told him he had three wishes. For his first wish…the Norwegian asked for a brand new red convertible, with all kinds of chrome and a terrific stereo and many other gadgets. Poof…instantly he was in a beautiful red convertible so gorgeous you wouldn't believe it. Then he said, "I wish I had a beautiful red haired gal in this car with me to help me enjoy it. Poof…instantly an absolutely ravishing, gorgeous young gal, right beside him. Then, he tuned in a station on his car radio. Beautiful music. As the song ended, a commercial came on. In his joy, the Norwegian began singing along with the commercial, "I wish I was an Oscar Mayer weiner…"

An oil drilling company in Texas had a big well fire. Even Red Adair couldn't put it out. They offered a reward of $50,000. A Norwegian fire department from Southern Texas offered to come up to try to put out the fire. As they came roaring up the highway, they turned off into the oil field . . . not only UP to the oil fire, but right IN it. The Norwegian firemen jumped out of their fire truck and began thrashing the fire with their jackets. Miraculously, the fire was put out by these Norwegians! As the superintendent reacted with amazement, he led Ole, the fire chief, into the company office where he made out a check for $50,000. "Congratulations, Ole," he said. "Here's your $50,000. Now, what do you plan to do with the money?" "Vell," said Ole, "first of all ve vill haff to get da brakes fixed on our fire truck."

■ ■ ■ ■

A Norwegian kid was delivering the newspaper to his new customer.
"What's your name, son?" inquired the customer.
"George Bush," said the kid.
"Well, that's a pretty well known name, isn't it?" remarked the customer.
"It oughta be," said the Norwegian youngster. "I've been delivering papers on dis route for over six months."

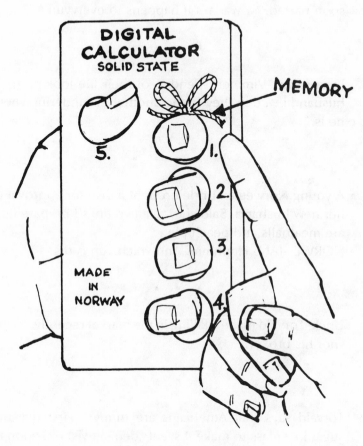

Norwegian Calculator

Ole say: "Dere vas a time ven a fool and his money were soon parted. Nowadays it happens to everyvun."

. . . .

Lena says: "Vimmen spend ⅓ of their life looking for a husband . . . den they spend another ⅔ vundering vhere he is."

. . . .

A young Norwegian bride brought a dish for approval of her new husband. Said she, "Da two tings I prepare best are meatballs and peach pie . . ."
NORWEGIAN: Hmmmm. And vhich vun is dis?

. . . .

Uncle Torvald made a killing in the market recently . . . he shot his broker.

. . . .

Torvald says that Americans are funny: "First day put sugar in a glass to make it sveet; den, a twist of lemon to make it sour, gin to make it varm dem up, and ice to cool it off. Den dey say, "Here's to you," and drink it demselves."

Torvald says: Bad news travels fast . . .
unless you mail it.

. . . .

Torvald asked the local banker, "Vots da latest dope on Wall Street?"
Answered the banker, sourly, "My son in law."

. . . .

Hjalmar, the fighter, was doing badly in the ring, having taken several nasty blows. He was finally put on the canvas by a right to the jaw. While the referee counted, Hjalmar's manager whispered, "Don't get up til eight." Hjalmar raised himself weakly and mumbled, "Vat time is it NOW?"

. . . .

Torvald comments: "A mortgage is a gimmick dat speeds up da months and slows down da years."

. . . .

Also from Torvald: "Scientists say dat man evolved from da monkey over several million years . . . but a voman can make a monkey out of a man in a couple seconds."

103

At the meeting of the Loyal Order of Norwegian Sons of Eric, the Secretary got up before the lodge to announce: "Tonight ve vill not be honored vid da presence of our most illustrious and powerful, all-seeing and omnipotent Grand Ruler of da Lodge. His vife von't let him out tonight."

. . . .

A carnival had come to town and the strong man was challenging the villagers in this Norwegian community. "I will squeeze this lemon," declared the strong man, "and if anyone can squeeze ONE drop more from it after I am done . . . he will be given one thousand dollars."

Several people tried it . . . but to no avail. Finally, a little, shriveled up guy stepped forward and said he'd like to try. The strong man squeezed a lemon with all his might, reducing it almost to pulp. Then he handed the remains to the little weak-looking man . . . who then squeezed and squeezed and squeezed . . . finally extracting ONE drop of lemon juice. The strong man was amazed, and while handing him the thousand dollars revealed that this was the first time he had had to forfeit the money. "Tell me, sir," said the strong man, "what do you do for a living?"

Said the little guy, in a quavering voice, "I'm the treasurer at the Norwegian Lutheran church."

A Norwegian appeared before the judge to have
his name changed.
"What is your name now?" asked the Judge.
"Ole Stinks," replied the Norwegian.
"Hmmm . . . I can see why you want it changed.
What do you want it changed to."
"Lars."

■ ■ ■ ■

How do Norwegians count?
"Vun, Two, Tree, Four, anudder, anudder,
anudder, anudder."

■ ■ ■ ■

Lars and Kari got divorced for religious reasons.
She worshipped money . . .
and he didn't have any.

■ ■ ■ ■

A knock on the door. Ole goes to answer it.
He encounters a masked man with a gun.
"Are you a robber?" inquires Ole.
"No . . . I'm a rapist."
Ole: "Lena . . . it's for you."

Torleiv was a cannon polisher at the court house for 20 years. Finally, when he had saved some money, he quit his job. Next thing that the people in the town heard . . . Torleiv had bought his own cannon. "Always wanted to go into business for myself," was his explanation.

■　■　■　■

Mikkelson was a traveling salesman and one day his car got stalled on a country road. A nearby farm house proved to be some Norwegians who invited him to stay the night. For supper, the menu included rommegrot. Although Mikkelson was crazy about rommegrot, he restrained himself and took only two helpings. At bedtime, the farmer explained they only had one bed, so Mikkelson would have to sleep between the farmer and his wife. About 3 in the morning, the farmer had to get up to tend to some farrowing sows. The farmer's wife tapped Mikkelson on the shoulder and whispered, "Now's your chance." So, Mikkelson tiptoed downstairs to the refrigerator and finished off the rommegrot!

■　■　■　■

Ole got in some trouble and was arraigned in court. The judge warned him, "Anything you say may be held against you."
"Oh boy," exclaimed Ole, "DOLLY PARTON, FARRAH FAUCETT, RAQUEL WELCH . . ."

KARL: Do you wake up grouchy?
OLE: No . . . I let her sleep.

．　．　．　．

Lars went to the doctor for a checkup. The doctor pronounced him fit as a fiddle for a man of 75 years. "How old was your father when he died?" inquired the doctor.

"Who says he's dead?" answered Lars. "He's 95 and in terrific shape. Rides a bike and golfs every day."

"Remarkable," commented the doctor. "How old was HIS father when he died?"

"Who says he's dead?" said Lars. "He's 120 years old and really in fantastic shape. Swims every day and goes bowling. In fact, he's getting married next week."

"Why in the world would a man of 120 years of age WANT to get married?" asked the doctor.

"He doesn't WANT to," answered Lars. "He HAS to."

．　．　．　．

Elofson, the undertaker, was hauling a corpse to the cemetery in Duluth, Minnesota. As the hearse was slowly progressing up the steep hill, the rear door accidentally came open and the casket, which was on rollers, went careening down the hill . . . with Elofson in hot pursuit. Just as the casket was heading into the door of a drugstore, Elofson ran breathlessly up to the druggist, gasping, "Say, Doc . . . have you got anything that will stop this coffin?"

OLE: What do you get when you mix holy water and prune juice?
KNUTE: Vell, I tink you get a religious movement.

• • • •

ARNIE: Say Torvald, I understand you and your wife celebrated your 25th anniversary last month. I suppose you had a party . . . killed a chicken or something?
TORVALD: No . . . ve vouldn't do dat. I don't believe in making a chicken suffer for something dat happened 25 years ago.

• • • •

PROFESSOR: In our experiment, we put a worm in water, and another worm in a glass of whiskey. Now . . . you see, the worm in the water is healthy, active and swimming around. On the other hand, the worm in the whiskey is already dead. Now, what does that prove to you?
OLE: Vell, it proves dat if you drink viskey . . . you won't have worms.

• • • •

The doctor told Lars he had six months to live. Lars said he couldn't pay the bill. So the Doctor gave him another six months.

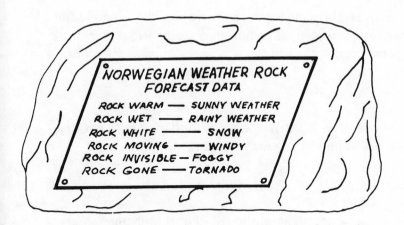

Make your own Norwegian Weather Rock

Why depend on unreliable TV forecasts?
Have your own never-fail method of determining
the weather.

∎ ∎ ∎ ∎

How do you get 20 Norwegians
into a Volkswagen?
—You throw a quarter into the back seat.

∎ ∎ ∎ ∎

OLE: What's the difference between a duck?
SVEN: I don't know.
OLE: One leg is both da same.

Ole and Lena made a good pair. He was knock kneed and she was bow legged. When they walked together, they spelled "OX".

. . . .

Ole says he wears dark glasses around the house because it bothers him to see his wife work so hard.

. . . .

More of same: "It's not the HIGH cost of living that gets us in trouble . . . it's the cost of HIGH LIVING."

. . . .

Magnus was inspecting little Hjalmar's report card. It was pretty grim. Finally, Magnus saw a bright note: "Vell, Hjalmar . . . vun ting in your favor . . . vid a report card like dis, it's a cinch you're not cheating."

. . . .

SVEN: Teacher, I don't tink I deserved a zero on dis test.
TEACHER: Neither do I . . . but it's the lowest grade I can give you.

Ole's brother, Rasmus was an over-the-hill boxer who refused to retire from the ring. After being knocked out for the 98th time, his manager began selling advertising space on the soles of his shoes.

. . . .

Ole was watching his poultry and the rooster was busy chasing the hens all over the chicken yard. Just for the heck of it, Ole took a hand full of corn and threw it in the rooster's path. The rooster immediately came to a screeching halt and commenced gobbling down the corn. "Boy," said Ole, "I hope I never get THAT hungry!"

. . . .

Wise sayings from Ole: "Any guy can have a wife . . . but only the Ice Man has his pick."

. . . .

DOCTOR: You seem to be healthy for a man of 75.
How is your love life?
KNUTE: Vell, almost every day.
DOCTOR: That's remarkable. Tell me more.
KNUTE: Vell, almost on Monday, almost on
Tuesday, almost on Vednesday, and so on.

LENA: Vhy do you go on da balcony vhen I sing?
Don't you like to hear me sing?
OLE: Vell, I yust vant da neighbors to see I'm
not beating my vife.

▪ ▪ ▪ ▪

Helga went down town to buy a single shoe to send to her son, Johan, who was in the army. (He'd written home that he'd grown another foot.).

▪ ▪ ▪ ▪

A Norwegian found a bottle on the street, rubbed it a bit to dust it off . . . suddenly a genie popped out, thanked the Norwegian, and told him he had three wishes. For his first wish . . . the Norwegian asked for a brand new red convertible, with all kinds of chrome and a terrific stereo and many other gadgets. Poof . . . instantly he was in a beautiful red convertible so gorgeous you wouldn't believe it. Then he said, "I wish I had a beautiful I red haired gal in this car with me to help me enjoy it. Poof . . . instantly an absolutely ravishing, gorgeous young gal, right beside him. Then, he tuned in a station on his car radio. Beautiful music. As the song ended, a commercial came on. In his joy, the Norwegian began singing along with the commercial, "I wish I was an Oscar Mayer weiner . . ."

SPEAKER: In this day and age, it is hazardous to use any jokes about ethnic groups. Many politicians and other public figures have gotten into trouble by using ethnic jokes. It is much safer to tell a story using a lost civilization like the Hittites. You've read about the Hittites in the Bible. They no longer exist. So, with your permission, I would like to tell you a story about two Hittites named Ole and Lars.

■　■　■　■

LARS: I heard that you had to shoot your dog, Fido. Was he mad?
OLE: Vell, he vasn't exactly pleased about it.

■　■　■　■

Torvald says that nowadays when he feels romantic he goes to bed with TWO women. "Dat vay," he explains, "if I fall asleep, dey can talk to each odder."

■　■　■　■

BRITA: I heard dat Ole proposed to you and dat you accepted. Did he tell you dat he had proposed to ME first?
LENA: Vell, no; but he did mention dat he had done a lot of foolish tings before ve met.

RALPH: Arnie, what's the difference
between ignorance and apathy?
ARNIE: I don't know . . . and I don't care!

• • • •

Lena went into a drug store and asked for
Talcum Powder.
Asked the druggist, "Mennens?"
"No, silly," said Lena . . . "Vimmens."

• • • •

Hans called Ole long distance and asked him
to loan him $5. "I can't hear you, Hans," said Ole.
"Dis line must be bad."
The operator broke in to say, "I can hear him
perfectly clear."
"Vell," said Ole, "If you can hear him so good,
vhy don't YOU lend him da five dollars."

• • • •

Rasmussen, who had a stuttering problem, was
expounding on the problems of the would. "I-I-I-I
tink-k-k dat ve S-s-s-h-o-u-ld Qv-v-v-v-it sending money
all-I-I-I- over da v-v-v-v-orld and Y-y-y-y-ust keep our
money t-t-t-t-t-o home."
"Oh, sure," snorted Kasperson . . . "Dat's easy for YOU
to say."

Hear about the Norwegian who disappeared?
He had just put on a pair of Odor Eaters.

. . . .

LENA: Ve don't know vhat to do vit Ole . . .
he tinks he's a chicken.
TENA: Vell den, you maybe should take him to
a psychiatrist. He needs help.
LENA: I know . . . but ve need da eggs.

. . . .

The teacher was writing some sentences on the black-board when she a dropped her chalk. As she bent over to pick it up, little Arnie piped up, "Teacher . . . I can see two inches above your knee." Outraged, the teacher said, "Arnie, for your impertinence, you are expelled from school for one week." Shortly, the teacher dropped the chalk again and bent over to pick it up. This time, little Ralph spoke up, "Teacher . . . I can see FOUR inches above your knee." Infuriated once again, the teacher ordered little Ralph to be expelled for TWO weeks. Ten minutes later the teacher once again dropped the chalk; and again, stooped over to pick it up. As she raised up, she noticed little Halvor grabbing his school books and heading toward the door. "Halvor, where are you going?" asked the teacher. Answered Halvor . . . "I'm going home, teacher, my school days are over."

HELGA: Vhat is a "Wooden Wedding?"
KNUTE: "I'm not sure . . . I tink dat is vhen
two Poles get married."

∎ ∎ ∎ ∎

A Norwegian had the misfortune while on a drinking
spree . . . to drink a quart of varnish. He died, of course.
But he had a beautiful finish.

∎ ∎ ∎ ∎

Ole has a digital alarm . . . Lena pokes him with a finger
to wake him.

∎ ∎ ∎ ∎

A Norwegian was bragging up America to his cronies in a
bar in Norway. "Yah, it is vunderful in America. You go
into a bar, have a few free drinks . . . den you go in da
back room and have free sex. Den you go back and have
some more free drinks . . . den you go back in da back
room and have more free sex. You can keep it up like dat
all night."
Sven was listening dubiously and remarked, "Ole, what
do you know about dese things . . . you've never been to
America?"
"I know," admitted Ole . . . "but my Sister has."

GENUINE NORWEGIAN WOOD STOVE

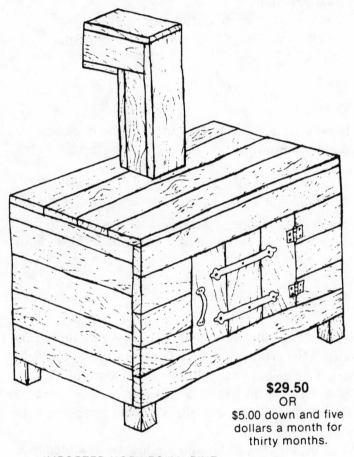

$29.50
OR
$5.00 down and five
dollars a month for
thirty months.

★ IMPORTED NORWEGIAN PINE
★ FIREPROOF, REUSABLE BRASS FIXTURES
★ GUARANTEED TO BURN OR YOUR MONEY BACK

Knute called the Salvation Army: "Do you save bad girls there?"

"Yes we do," came the answer.

"Vell," said Knute . . . "save me vun for Saturday night."

. . . .

Ole calls his dog CARPENTER. Because he does odd jobs around the house.

. . . .

A Swedish woman sent her husband downtown to buy a Lazy Boy rocker. He came back with a Norwegian guitar player.

. . . .

Ole was spending some time in Dodge City during the frontier days. He stalked into a saloon yelling, "All right, vhere is da galoot vhat painted my horse purple?"

"Right HERE!" answered a vicious looking cowpoke standing about seven feet tall. "What are you going to do about it?"

"Nutting," answered Ole with a gulp, "I yust vanted to let you know dat da first coat is dry."

LARS: Vaitress . . . bring me some vatery scram-
bled eggs, den burn some toast,
den bring me some veak coffee.
WAITRESS: Yes sir, right away.
LARS: Don't be too fast . . . and vhile you're at it . . .
nag me awhile . . . I'm homesick for my vife.

．　．　．　．

KNUTE: Caddy . . . how would you haff played
dat last shot?
CADDY: Under an assumed name.

．　．　．　．

Ole and Lars were shipwrecked on a small island in the
Pacific. Also stranded was an Irishman named Kelly. As
time went on, the men grew accustomed to being
marooned and led a good life on the island. Finally, the
Irishman died. The two Norwegians were puzzled about
how to give Kelly a proper funeral since he had been a
Catholic. Ole volunteered to do the service if Lars would
dig the grave. Ole said he had once listened to a Catholic
church service, so after Lars dug a big hole, Ole put on his
best ministerial tone: "In da name of da Father, the son,
and (shoving Kelly's body with a foot) IN DA HOLE HE
GOES!"

Lena went back to Norway to visit her sister.
Back home, Ole was keeping house by himself.
Lars asked him if he was lonesome all by
himself.
"Vell, a little," said Ole. "But vunce a veek, I
have a voman come in and nag."

■ ■ ■ ■

Ole and Lena took little Lars to church for the first time.
After the services, they asked him how he liked it. "Vell,"
said little Lars, "Da music program was OK, but da commercial vas too long."

■ ■ ■ ■

Svenson was an incurable optimist. No matter what
horrible event people would tell him about, Svenson
would invariably say, "Vell, it could have been
worse." One day two of his cronies told Svenson
about the terrible tragedy where Bjarne Olsson was
killed by Olaf Hegermoe after Bjarne had been fooling around with Hegermoe's wife.
"Vell," said Sevenson in his usual manner, "It could
have been vorse." "Vorse? How could it have been
vorse?" asked the crony. "Vell," said Svenson, "If it
had been da night before, it vould have been ME."

Why are Norwegian mothers so strong?
From raising dumb-bells.

. . . .

You've heard about bad cooks . . .
Lena actually keeps Alka Seltzer on TAP.

. . . .

Bakkedahl was musing on the park bench. "Vunce I had everything . . . a nice apartment . . . the love of a tender young voman. And den my vife had to valk in and spoil it."

. . . .

Lars says, "I married my vife because of a mental problem.
I vas out of my mind at da time."

. . . .

Ole and Lena were going home from the grocery store with Ole pushing the baby carriage.
Suddenly Lena exclaimed:
"Ole . . . we've got da wrong baby!"
"SSHHH" said Ole . . . "dis is a better buggy."

A Norwegian was dickering on a new Cadillac. The salesman told him it would cost $16,000, but if he could decide that day, he would be allowed 10% off. The Norwegian, not being willing to admit he couldn't figure such high mathematics, told the salesman he'd have to think it over for a few minutes. So he walked across the street to a cafe. He sat sipping on coffee, trying to figure it out with a pencil and paper. Finally, about to give up, he called the waitress over to see if she could help him. "Say, Vaitress," said the Norwegian, "How much vould you take off for 10 percent of $16,000?" The waitress grinned and asked demurely, "Would my earrings get in the way?"

■ ■ ■ ■

Ole once had an implement dealership in Wisconsin. His motto was: "Ve stand behind all of our implements . . . vid de exception of da manure spreader."

■ ■ ■ ■

This Norwegian lived way, way out in the woods in Minnesota . . . seldom came into town. Finally when the snow went out, the Norwegian and his wife went to Duluth. They spent nearly two hours watching a microwave oven. Finally, the Norwegian got up in disgust. "Come on, Ma," he said, "If dis is vat television is like, dey can have it."

NORWEGIAN SNO-MOBILE

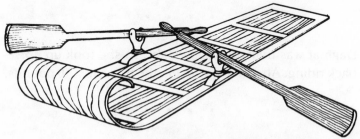

**SPECIAL DELUX MODEL
ONLY
$49.50 Plus Tax**

A Norwegian was recently arrested for passing bogus $2 bills. The way he did it was to erase the zero from $20 bills.

. . . .

The Norwegians are planning to launch a space flight to the sun. When asked by a reporter how they planned to avoid burning up, a Norwegian spokesman answered, "Ve figure on going at night."

A Norwegian calls up his Doctor and says, "Every morning at 5 I have a B.M."
"Fine," said the Doctor. "That's very healthy. What seems to be your problem?"
"Vell," said the Norwegian. "I don't vake up 'till six."

■ ■ ■ ■

Dagmar was trying to lose weight, so she took up horse-back riding. After the first week, the horse lost 10 pounds.

■ ■ ■ ■

MOMMA JOHNSON: Eat your spinach, Hjalmar. It'll put color in your cheeks.
Hjalmar: Who vants green cheeks.

■ ■ ■ ■

Lars say, "No vun can say I'm a quitter . . . I stay on the job 'til I get fired."

■ ■ ■ ■

Ole says, "I never get mad vhen I play golf . . . if I miss a shot, I yust laugh. Yesterday I laughed 115 times."

Two Norwegians were building a house. One of them reached into a sack of nails and said, "Lars, you got us the wrong kind of nails. Dese nails have got the point on the wrong end."

"Dat's okay," said Lars, "Ve can use dem on the other side of the house."

•   •   •   •

Ole says: "Be very careful ven a guy tells you he is boss at home. Some day he might lie to you about sumting important."

•   •   •   •

Sven was flying on an airliner when the plane encountered extremely turbulent conditions. A nervous old lady, expecting disaster, turned around to Sven and implored, "Please do something religious." So, Sven started a Bingo game.

•   •   •   •

Ole Torkelson is quite a clown . . . always joking. Even in the hospital. When he was laid up in the hospital and someone knocked at the door, he'd call out, "Who goes dere . . . friend or enema?"

ODE TO DA NORVEGIANS
by Julie Stangeland

Vel, da Svedes, dey got a lot of ham
Vich means a lot of hogs,
And da Danes, dey got a million of
Dose great big whopping dogs.

And da Finns, dey got da reindeer
And dey got da sheep and cows,
But da Norskies had dose Wiking ships
Vit dragons on da prows.

Dey used dem to go pilla-ying;
Dey'd land and den say, "Hi!
Say, vere's da gold and silver?
Hand it over now, or fry!"

And ven dey got to England,
Dis is vat dey did:
Dey left behind deir nouns and werbs
And lots of liddle kids.

Dey conquered everybody in
Da vorld, and den, to boot,
Dey even got dese real svell names
Like Olaf, Sven and Knute.

So dat's my Norskie poem
And it makes me feel so sad
Dat everyvun can't be Norvegian
Yust like my dear old Dad.

126

Ole met a guy the other day
who is half Norwegian
and half Palestinian Arab.
His name? "Yasser Yubetcha."

• • • •

Ole says, "It's a shame dat all da folks who REALLY know
how to run da country are all driving cabs or cutting hair."

• • • •

MARI: You look like a million dollars.
KARL: How's dat?
MARI: Green and wrinkled.

• • • •

Here are a couple of Norwegian jokes exported (or was it
"**de**ported"?) from Norway.

Rolf Liland, who hails from Hop, Norway, asks:
"How can you identify the pessimistic Norwegian at the
air field?"
He's the one without a ripchord on his parachute because
he figures it won't open anyway.
And the Norwegian optimist jumps without a parachute
because he figures he can borrow one on the way down.

HELGA: I bought dis dress for a ridiculous figure.
KARI: Vell, YOU said it . . . not me.

■   ■   ■   ■

Also from Ole: "Vimmen get married so day can make a homing pigeon out of a night Owl."

■   ■   ■   ■

Lars was released from his employment so he asked for a letter of recommendation. The boss wrote: "Lars worked for us for five years. He is no longer working for us. We are very satisfied."

■   ■   ■   ■

Uncle Torvald explains what happens when you cross a gorilla with a computer: "You get a Hairy Reasoner."

■   ■   ■   ■

Torvald might be considered a little simple . . . he thinks that Assets are little donkeys.

■   ■   ■   ■

Ole says: "Never tell people your troubles. Half of dem don't care . . . and da odder half is glad it happened to you."

Ole was reading the paper. "Lena," he said, "dis is really interesting. De bathtub vas invented in 1850 and da telephone vasn't invented until 1875. Yust tink...a guy could have spent twenty-five years in da bath tub vidout da phone ringing VUNCE."

Ole was sent to prison for one year because he was caught taking some hogs that belonged to a neighbor. The day he left the farm to go to prison was a sad one. As he bravely bid goodbye to Lena, he said, "Lena, I'm leaving you and da hired man in charge of da farm til I get back."

Upon his release, Ole happily came back to the farm where he found things in good condition and the farm thriving. Even Lena seemed in fairly good spirits as she greeted him after his 12 months away. Lena served Ole some of his favorite lutefisk and lefse. As Ole gazed around the kitchen, he spotted a jar in the cupboard with 9 dollars and five soybeans in it.

"Lena," he queried, "Vhat is dat yar vid five soybeans in it?" "Oh, Ole," said Lena, "I have a confession to make. Vhen you vas in prison, I got awfly lonesome vidout you. So vhen I couldn't stand it so good, da hired man and me, vell, ve kinda got togetdder a few times. And vhen ve did, ve put a soybean in da yar."

Ole thought a minute, and told himself that in a year's time, five occasions weren't so bad that he couldn't forgive Lena. "But Lena," said Ole, "Vhat is da nine dollars for?"

"Vell, you see, vun day da market on soybeans vas up to nine dollars, so I yust sold off a bushel."

There was a Norwegian who was so dumb he ran downtown to get wheels for his wife's menstrual cycle.

• • • •

News item from OSLO: "The police here have arrested a Norwegian for selling 'Eternal Youth' pills. Records at the Oslo police station showed he was a repeat offender. He has been similarly charged in 1452, 1799, and 1935."

• • • •

A Norwegian got on a TV quiz program. Said the Quizmaster, "and now for $20,000 . . . can you tell me . . . HOW MANY D'S in "Here Comes the Bride?"
The Norwegian scratched his head, shifted his weight from one foot to the other, gazed at the ceiling, and finally declared, "68."
"68?" exclaimed the Quizmaster. That is incorrect. But how did you arrive at 68?
The Norwegian answered by humming, "De De de de . . . De de de de . . . ."

• • • •

Jens is on a new diet.
He never eats while his wife is talking.

131

Lena was in the bathtub when the door bell rang.
"Who iss it?" she called out.
"Blind man," came the answer from the front door.
Lena got out of the tub, walked straight to the
front door without so much as a stitch of clothes,
and threw open the door.
There stood a man who asked, "Where do you
want me to put these blinds, lady?"

■   ■   ■   ■

JOHAN: You say it mentions tennis in da Bible.
Vhere does it say dat?
HALVOR: I forget where it is exactly . . .
but it does mention dat Joseph served
in Pharaoh's court.

■   ■   ■   ■

Katrina was in her car, stopped at a traffic light. The light
turned red, green, amber, and then red again. A cop
standing on the corner was heard to comment, "Lady, let
me know when you see a color you like."

■   ■   ■   ■

Knute claims that the first actor in history was Samson:
"He brought down da house," comments Knute.

Did you hear about the Norwegian who couldn't spell very well?
—He spent all night in a WAREHOUSE.

. . . .

Two Norwegians hi-jacked a submarine . . . then demanded $100,000 and two parachutes.

. . . .

A Norwegian in our town took a bus trip from Wisconsin to California. He had to rest up for a couple of days due to "bus-lag."

. . . .

A Norwegian girl went into a drug store and asked for talcum powder.
"Yes maam . . . walk this way," said the druggist, walking briskly down the aisle.
"Uff Da," said the girl. "If I could valk **dat** vay, I vouldn't need da talcum powder."

. . . .

What do you call a Norwegian education?
—"Trivial Pursuit."

An itinerant lawyer named Blaine Nels Simons was working on a case in a rural community. When his car broke down, he was forced to borrow a horse from a country preacher, Rev. Donald Anderson. The preacher gave Simons instructions on how to make the horse go and stop. "First, you say, 'Praise the Lord', and the horse will go. And to make him stop, just say, 'Amen'." So the lawyer started on his journey by saying, "Praise the Lord." And sure enough, the horse took off. In fact, on a fast gallop. This startled the lawyer to such an extent that when he began panicking because of the horse's speed, he forgot the word to make him stop. Just as the horse was careening toward a cliff, and appeared about to go over the cliff, the lawyer suddenly remembered the word, "Amen." And sure enough, the horse stopped right at the cliff's edge. With a huge sigh of relief, the lawyer mopped his brow and fervently uttered, "PRAISE THE LORD!"

■　■　■　■

OLE SAYS . . . You Know You're Getting Old When . . .

Everything hurts and what doesn't hurt, doesn't work.
Your little black book contains only names
ending in M.D.
Your children begin to look middle aged.
You're still chasing women but can't remember why.
You know all the answers, but nobody asks you the questions.

Norwegian Ambush

Ole and Lars worked on a construction crew. One day Lars noticed that the foreman always left the project about an hour early. "Say Ole," suggested Lars. "Why don't WE take off a little early too . . . yust like da foreman." So they agreed to try it. As soon as Ole got home, he looked all over for Lena. Finally he opened the bedroom door . . . and there she was in bed with the foreman. Ole silently closed the door and tiptoed out of the house. The next day he confronted Lars. "Ve better not try anudder stunt like ve did yesterday. I almost got caught."

FOUR

UFF DA JOKES

THE MEANING OF "UFF DA"

"Uff Da" is not in the dictionary, but for many Scandinavians, it is an all-purpose expression covering a variety of situations such as:

Uff Da is . . . the same as Charlie Brown's "Good Grief."

Uff Da is . . . looking in the mirror and discovering . . . you're not getting better, you're just getting older.

Uff Da is . . . trying to dance the polka to rock and roll music.

Uff Da is . . . losing your wad of gum in the chicken yard.

Uff Da is . . . eating hot soup when you've got a runny nose.

Uff Da is . . . waking yourself up in church with your own snoring.

Uff Da is . . . sneezing so hard that your false teeth end up in the bread plate.

Uff Da is . . . walking all the way downtown and then trying to remember what you wanted.

Uff Da is . . . getting swished in the face with a cow's wet tail.

Uff Da is . . . trying to pour two buckets of manure into one bucket.

Uff Da is . . . eating a delicious sandwich and then discovering the spread is cat food.

Uff Da is . . . arriving late at a lutefisk supper and getting served minced ham instead.

Uff Da is . . . when your two "steady" girl friends find out about each other.

Uff Da is . . . trying to look at yourself in the mirror January 1st.

Uff Da is . . . looking in your rear view mirror and seeing flashing red lights.

Uff Da is . . . pushing the light switch and suddenly remembering you forgot to pay the electric bill.

Uff Da is . . . opening up the latest real estate tax bill.

Uff Da is . . . noticing non-Norwegians at a church dinner using lefse for a napkin.

Uff Da is . . . watching what dogs do to lutefisk piled up in front of the butcher shop.

Uff Da is . . . not being Scandinavian.

A Swede in Minnesota decided to have himself cloned and the result was a perfect likeness of himself in every detail except one. And that was the Clone had a filthy mouth . . . making obscene remarks wherever he went, much to the extreme embarrassment of the Swede. Finally, it had such a damaging effect on the Swede's life with the rotten-talking Clone ruining his reputation that the Swede invited the Clone to go on an outing to the countryside.

The Swede enticed the clone to view the magnificent scenery from the edge of a cliff, or bluff as they are called in Minnesota. As the Clone leaned forward to glimpse the panorama below, the Swede quickly bumped him from behind and the Clone fell over the 120 foot precipice to the rocks below. When the Swede surmised that death had occurred, he got in his car and went back to town. Several days went by and he figured that when the body was found, it would be presumed an accident with no blame toward him. But one day two policemen walked in and arrested the Swede.

Why?

For making an obscene Clone fall.

■　■　■　■

In our town there is a Norwegian who found himself locked in his car, and had to break three windows before he could get out.

Ole was a businessman, and one day got a request from the government to fill out a form about his employees. One question asked: "How many employees do you have broken down by sex?" When Ole filled out the answer, he wrote; "Practically all of dem."

■ ■ ■ ■

Capt. Ragnar Folven from Sandnes tells about two Norwegians sitting in a park, one reading a newspaper. The other asks, "What date is it today?" To which the other responds, "I don't know." "But," says the first Norwegian, "can't you look in your paper?" "It's no use," says the other. "This is yesterday's paper."

■ ■ ■ ■

Ole was out of work and in looking for a job, applied at the Dingaling Brothers Circus. The circus manager looked Ole over from head to toe, and then disclosed that they might be able to use Ole in the Human Cannonball act. "I think you'd work out fine, Ole," said the manager. "We could use a man of your caliber."

■ ■ ■

A Norwegian got married and on the wedding night his bride disrobed and suggested, "Get aboard, Ole." By the time Ole got back from the lumber yard, the bride had fallen asleep.

A Norwegian drove in front of the Cadillac agency in a brand new Cadillac. "Where's your service department?" he asked.

"Service department?" exclaimed the dealer. "You have a brand new Cadillac. You don't need service on it yet, surely?"

"Vell," said the Norwegian. "Ay been used to da stick shift . . . and this car has got those funny letters like PRNDL on the steering veel."

"Yes, that's correct," said the dealer. "That's the automatic transmission."

"Vell," said the Norwegian. "I first put 'er in 'L' for 'light out.' Den I see a guy trying to pass. So I put 'er in 'S' for 'Sic 'em.' Dat put me a little faster. So when anodder car starts to pass, I looks at the dial and put 'er in 'D' for 'Dig in.' Boy, I really got going. All of a sudden a kid in a hot rod started to go 'round me. So I looked at the dial again and put it in 'R' for 'Racing'."

"Where's your service department?"

This is a sign hung in Ole's Cafe in Decorah:
Please don't criticize da coffee.
You may be old and veak someday yourself.

. . . .

A nurse in the hospital came out to the waiting room to tell the Norwegian that his wife had just had a baby. "I'm happy to tell you that you have a little girl," said the nurse, "but I'm sorry that I have to tell you that one leg is a bit shorter than the other."
"Vell, dat's all right," responded the Norwegian.
"Ve vere planning to call her 'Eileen' anyvay."

. . . .

Here are three wise Old Norwegian sayings:

1. Never eat at a place called "Mom's"
2. Never play cards with a guy named "Doc."
3. Never buy fresh fish from a truck with Oklahoma license plates.

. . . .

The Swede called on his girl friend and his shirt was dripping wet. When asked why he replied,
"The label said 'Wash and Wear'."

The Norwegian government recently purchased 1,000 used septic tanks; and as soon as they learn how to drive them, they plan to invade Sweden.

■ ■ ■ ■

We know a Norwegian who's so dumb that he thinks a can opener is a key to the bathroom.

■ ■ ■ ■

DANE: What would you do if you found
a million dollars?
SWEDE: Vell, if it belonged to a poor person,
I'd return it.

■ ■ ■ ■

A Norwegian discovered he had mice in the house, so he set a trap. Being a bit thrifty, he used as bait . . . a picture of a piece of cheese. When he checked the trap next morning he found . . . a picture of a mouse!

■ ■ ■ ■

Did you hear about the Norwegian who thought that Manual Labor was the President of Mexico?

Ole's friend, Lars, says, "Single people die earlier. Marriage is healthier. So, if you're looking for a long life and a slow death, get MARRIED."

■ ■ ■ ■

Ole says, "Prices are getting so high dat da only vuns dat can make a deposit on a new car are da PIGEONS."

■ ■ ■ ■

Hjalmar went to see a lawyer about a divorce from his wife, Tina.

The lawyer began asking some questions.

"What grounds do you have?" he asked.

"Grounds?" said Hjalmar.

"Vell, ve got about half an acre vid da house."

"No, I mean, do you have a grudge?"

Said Hjalmar, "Ya, ve got a single car grudge back of da house."

The lawyer shook his head and continued, "Well, does she beat you up?"

"No, I usually get up about 6 and she stays in bed til about 7."

Getting a bit impatient, the lawyer finally asked, "Is she a nagger?"

"No," answered Hjalmer..."she's yust a Norvegian."

Norwegian Adjustable Dog Carrier

You Know You're Getting Old When . . .

You look forward to a dull evening.
You walk with your head high trying to get used to your bifocals.
Your favorite part of the newspaper is 25 years ago today.
You turn out the light for economic rather than romantic reasons.
You sit in a rocking chair and can't get it going.
Your knees buckle and your belt won't.
You regret all those mistakes resisting temptation.
You're 17 around the neck, 42 around the waist, and 96 around the golf course.
After painting the town red, you have to take a long rest before applying a second coat.
Dialing long distance wears you out.
You remember today that your wedding anniversary was yesterday.
You can't stand people who are intolerant.
The best part of your day is over when your alarm clock goes off.
You burn the midnight oil until 9 P.M.
Your back goes out more often than you do.
A fortune teller offers to read your face.
Your pacemaker makes the garage door go up when you watch a pretty girl go by.
The little gray-haired lady you help across the street is your wife.

OLE: Call da manager . . . I can't eat dis food.
WAITRESS: It's no use . . . he won't eat it either.

∎ ∎ ∎ ∎

Dagfinn loved crossword puzzles. When he died, his last request was to be buried 6 down and 3 across.

∎ ∎ ∎ ∎

OLE: (Talking about Lena) Yah, she's yust like an angel. Alvays up in da air and harping about sum-ting.

∎ ∎ ∎ ∎

The judge had just awarded a divorce to Lena who had charged non-support. He said to Ole, "I have decided to give your wife $400 a month for support." "Vell, dat's fine, Judge," said Ole. "And vunce in a while I'll try to chip in a few bucks myself."

∎ ∎ ∎ ∎

INGRID: Vould you like to see da ring dat Lars gave me?
HELGA: It looks like a nice ring. And it must be a comfort to know dat he isn't a spend-thrift.

147

What did they call the Swede who was half Indian? "Running Dummy."

• • • •

Lars says: "Gunderson must have a kidney condition . . . everytime dey bring da check in a restaurant, he has to go to da men's room.

• • • •

Ole and Lars were business partners and good friends. One day Lars started off for work and discovered he'd forgotten his tools. Returning home, he looked around for his wife, Lena, and finally found her in the bedroom. To his surprise, she was on the bed with no clothes on. "Vat in the vorld are you doing vidout any clothes, voman?" Lars asked.

"Vell, I yust don't have any clothes to vear, dat's vhy," answered Lena.

"Vat you talking about," said Lars as he opened the closet door and began counting: "Vun dress, two dress, tree dress, four dress . . . hello Ole . . . five dress . . .

• • • •

A Norwegian in our town was apprehended for stealing a lady's underskirt from the clothes line. The judge let him off, however, because "It was his first slip."

148

THE STORY OF OLE OLSON

Ole Olson was the janitor in the First Lutheran Church in Minneapolis. A new minister decreed that all employees should be able to read and write English. The reasoning was that all employees should be able to handle phone calls and write down information for the minister in his absence. Poor Ole! He had left Norway in his youth and never had learned to read and write. Despite his tearful pleas to the minister, Ole was forced to leave his job as Janitor because of his lack of education.

In his bitter disappointment, Ole hitch hiked to Seattle and got a job in a fish cannery. No worry about reading and writing here. He later worked on a fishing boat, and in time saved enough to buy his own boat.

As time passed, Ole acquired many more boats . . . in fact, a fishing fleet. With pyramiding profits and Ole's natural thrift, Ole eventually became owner of a small fish cannery in addition to his sizeable fleet of boats.

Then came the opportunity to buy a much larger cannery in Seattle. For the first time in his life, Ole was forced to consider going to a bank because the amount involved was much more than he could handle from his cash reserves.

As Ole recited his list of impressive assets, the banker smiled and assured Ole the loan would be granted. The loan papers were handed to Ole to sign. Said Ole, "I'm sorry . . . but I don't know how to read or write."

The astounded banker looked at Ole in disbelief. "Mr. Olson...it is necessary for you to sign to make this loan legal. I am astounded at your assets. Just where would you be today IF you could read and write?"

"Vell," said Ole, "I'd probably be a yanitor in the Lutheran Church in Minneapolis."

■ ■ ■ ■

KARI: Ole, you remind me of da ocean.
OLE: You mean...vild, restless and romantic?
KARI: No...you make me sick!

■ ■ ■ ■

Ole received a notice in the mail from his employer that he was being laid off from his job. The boss was surprised a few days later to see Ole at the factory gate. "Ole," he said, "I thought I sent you a notice that you were laid off." "Yah, dat's right boss...but on da envelope it says, 'Return in Five days to Yohnson's Pickle Factory.' So here I am."

■ ■ ■ ■

Lena says grocery shopping is getting to be just like a religious experience. She says, "All you see is people going up and down da aisles, and ven day see da prices, dey all say, "O MY GOD. O MY GOD."

150

St. Urho's Day

On March 16, the annual celebration of St. Urho's Day, we would like to acquaint those of you who may not be aware of the famous St. Urho, with the details of his legendary life and his rise to fame and finally the honor of being noted as the Patron Saint of all Good Finns! In order to do this, we Finns delved deeply into the archives to come up with the following description of that most auspicious day . . .

One of the lesser known, but extraordinary legends of ages past is the legend of St. Urho. He is the patron saint of the Finnish vineyard workers. This legend goes back before the last glacial period when wild grapes grew in abundance in the area now known as Finland. Archeologists have uncovered evidence of this scratched on the thigh bones of the giant bears that once roamed northern Europe. The wild grapes were threatened by a plague of grasshoppers until St. Urho banished the lot of them with a few select words.

In memory of this impressive demonstration of the Finnish language, Finnish people (and a few selected others) celebrate on March 16th (the day before St. Patrick's Day). At sunrise on March 16, Finnish women and children dressed in royal purple and nile green, gather around the shores of the many lakes in Finland and Chant what St. Urho chanted many years ago: "Heinsirkka, Heinsirkka, mena Taalta Hiiteen!" (Grasshopper, grasshopper, go away!)

151

Adult males, dressed in green costumes, gather on the hills overlooking the lakes, listen to the chant and then kicking out like grasshoppers, they slowly disappear to change costumes from green to purple. The celebration ends with singing and dancing polkas and schottisches. Everyone drinks grape juice (fermented??) to celebrate the occasion. Note: The color for the day is royal purple and nile green, and the accepted beverage is grape juice (of any alcoholic content desired). Or, an alternative, any good Finn would accept a Grasshopper as a substitute for grape juice.

And finally, as a salute to St. Urho from the northern Minnesota Finns:

Ooksi, Kooksie, coolama vee,
Santia Urho is ta poy for me!
He sase out ta hoppers as pig as birds,
Neffer peefor haff I hurd does words!

He reely told does pugs of kreen,
Braffest Finn I effer seen.
Some celebrate St. Pat unt hiss snakes,
Putt urho poyka got what it takes!

He got all tall and trong from fellia sour,
Unt ate culla moyakka effery hour.
Tat's why dat guy could sase does peetles,
What crew as tick as chack pine needles!

So let's give a cheer in hower pest vay,
On the sixteenth of March, St. Urho's Tay!!

"THE UFF DA BOOK" TREASURY OF EXOTIC RECIPES OF THE SCANDINAVIAN KIND

Even though the rest of this book is humorously inclined, we will get serious long enough to impart the condensed culinary secrets of the Scandinavian people. We begin with, naturally.

LUTEFISK: (BOILING) Before using, wash the lutefisk. After removing the dark skin, cut into serving size pieces. Place into cheese cloth bag and put in kettle of cold salted water. Bring to boil and cook about 5 minutes, or until tender. Serve with melted butter or cream sauce.

LEFSE:

5 large potatoes	3 T butter
½ cup sweet cream	1 tsp. salt

Flour, ½ cup per cup of mashed potatoes

Boil and mash the potatoes—add cream, butter and salt; beat until light, then cool. Add the flour, roll into a ball and knead until smooth. Cut into pieces about the size of an egg. Roll round, like pie crust, and very thin. Bake on large griddle to light tan. Moderate heat . . . do not scorch! Do not grease griddle. When baked, place between wax paper to prevent drying. Cut lefse into halves or quarters to serve. Serve with butter and sugar . . . possibly with cinnamon or preserves of your choice.

EBLESKIVER [DANISH FRIED CAKES]:

1½ cups flour
1 teaspoon baking
   powder
½ teaspoon soda

¼ teaspoon salt
2 eggs, beaten
2 cups sour cream
   or buttermilk

METHOD: Sift dry ingredients into bowl, add liquid and eggs and beat until smooth. Heat ebleskive pan, put 1 teaspoon melted butter into each hole, then fill half full of batter. When light brown, turn with fork and brown on other side; use rather low heat so inside of ebleskive will be done. Serve with sugar or jam. Cooked apples may be put on top of batter before turning to brown other side.

SOT SUPPE [Norwegian Sweet Soup]

1 cup prunes
1 cup seedless raisins
½ cup currants
1 cup chopped apples
2 cups grape juice

3 cups water
1 cup sugar
½ cup minute tapioca
1 stick cinnamon
¼ teaspoon salt

METHOD: Combine all ingredients except grape juice and cook until fruit is tender. Then, add grape juice and ½ lemon sliced. Serve hot with rusks. May be served cold as dessert—garnish with whipped cream and chopped nuts.

KRUM KAKE:

3 eggs, beaten well
1½ cup sugar
1 cup melted butter
1½ cups milk

1 tsp. baking powder
1 tsp. vanilla
2 cups (scant) flour

Bake on Krum Kake iron, 1 teaspoon at a time; roll while hot. Fill with whipped cream if desired.

FRIKADELLER [DANISH MEAT BALLS]

1 pound cooked beef
¼ pound salt pork
1 onion

4 eggs, beaten
2 cups milk
1 slice dry bread

Salt and pepper

METHOD: Grind meat, salt pork and onion together. Soften bread in milk and add with rest of ingredients to meat mixture. Shape into meat balls. Beat one egg and mix with 1 cup finely crushed cracker crumbs. Coat the meat balls well with crumb mixture and fry in hot butter slowly, turning to brown well.

Joke Bonus
A Norwegian is someone who on Easter will dye Easter eggs white.

A Norwegian sent his son to college. In his second year the boy got a girl in trouble. The fast thinking lad wrote to his dad, saying that a professor at the school could teach old Shep to talk for $1,000. Impressed, the Norwegian sent the money and shipped old Shep to the boy. A few months later, the boy committed the same indiscretion, so he wrote the old man again with the claim that the same professor could teach old Shep to read. Again the old man came through with $1,000, feeling that a talking dog should be able to read. At the close of the school year, the Norwegian went to the depot to meet his son coming in on the train. Lo and behold, THERE was the boy . . . but no old Shep! "Where's old Shep, Son?" asked the father. Again, the fast thinking boy had an answer. "Ya know, Dad, two nights ago old Shep and I were having a chat while he was reading the paper. I said it sure would be good to come back home, and Shep said, yeh, he missed the folks and farm. And he said he wondered if the old man was still fooling around with the hired girl. And you know, Dad, I got so mad at that remark that I reached over and choked that old dog. Before I could control myself, old Shep had died."

Quickly the father leaned forward and asked anxiously, "Are you sure that dog is dead, Son?"

■ ■ ■ ■

EYE DOCTOR: "Have your eyes
ever been checked?"
DANE: "No . . . they've always been plain blue."

156

"O LUTEFISK"
(May be sung to the tune of "O Tannenbaum")

O Lutefisk . . . O Lutefisk . . . how fragrant your aroma
O Lutefisk . . . O Lutefisk . . . You put me in a coma.
You smell so strong . . . you look like glue
You taste yust like an overshoe
But Lutefisk . . . come Saturday
I tink I'll eat you anyvay.

O Lutefisk . . . O Lutefisk . . . I put you by the door vay
I vanted you to ripen up . . . yust like dey do in Norvay
A dog came by and sprinkled you . . .
I hit him vid an army shoe
O Lutefisk . . . now I suppose
I'll eat you as I hold my nose.

O Lutefisk . . . O Lutefisk . . . how vell I do remember
On Christmas eve how we'd receive . . .
our big treat of December
It vasn't turkey or fried ham . . .
it vasn't even pickled spam
My mudder knew dere vas no risk . . .
In serving buttered lutefisk.

O Lutefisk . . . O Lutefisk . . . now everyone discovers
Dat Lutefisk and lefse makes . . .
Norvegians better lovers
Now all da vorld can have a ball . . .
you're better dan dat Yeritol
O Lutefisk . . . vid brennevin
You make me feel like Errol Flynn.

Norwegian Navel Salute

HISTORY OF ST. PATRICK'S DAY

St. Patrick's Day is celebrated on March 17th in commemoration of that historical figure's act of driving the Norwegians out of Ireland.

It seems that centuries ago, many Norwegians came to Ireland to escape the bitterness of the Norwegian winters. Ireland was having a famine at the time and food was very scarce.

The Norwegians were eating almost all the fish caught in the sea, leaving the Irish with nothing but potatoes. St. Patrick, taking things into his own hands, decided the Norwegians had to go. Secretly, he organized the IRATRION (Irish Republic Army to Rid Ireland of Norwegians). Irish members of IRATRION sabotaged all the power plants in hopes the fish the Norwegians kept in refrigerators would spoil, forcing the Norwegians to a colder climate where their fish would keep. The fish spoiled, all right, but the Norwegians, as everyone knows, thrive on spoiled fish.

Faced with failure, the Irish sneaked into the Norwegians' fish storage caves in the dead of night and sprinkled the rotten fish with lye, hoping to poison the Norwegian intruders. But, miraculously, the Norwegians thrived on this new concoction and dubbed the smelly lye-soaked fish "Lutefisk."

Matters became even worse for the Irishmen when the Norwegians started taking over the Irish potato crop and making lefse. Poor St. Patrick was at his wits end, and finally on March 17th, he blew his top and told the Norwegians to go to Hell, and it worked. All the Norwegians left Ireland and moved to Minnesota.

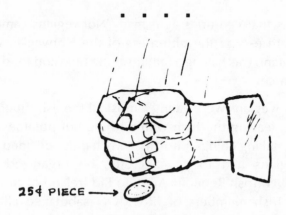

Norwegian Quarter Pounder

As you may know, Norway is the new Oil Kingdom with off-shore drilling bringing millions if not billions to the country. A publication sent to us from Norway tells of how the Swedes have been telling jokes about Norwegians on the oil platforms throwing breadcrumbs at the helicopters. But the Norwegians had a comeback, telling how the Swedish helicopter pilots swoop down to pick up the bread crumbs.

Q. Where do the Swedes keep their armies?
A. Up their sleevies.

•   •   •   •

A smart Norwegian, a dumb Norwegian and Santa Claus started walking toward a $20 bill.
Which one got it?
The dumb Norwegian. The other two are fictional.

•   •   •   •

A Danish lady sent her husband downtown
to get a pair of loafers.
So he came back with two Norwegians.

•   •   •   •

A Norwegian reached retirement age and found too much time on his hands. So, a friend suggested he get a hobby, like raising chickens. The Norwegian went to a hatchery and bought 200 chicks. The next week he came back and bought 200 more. After another week, he came to the hatchery once more to order 200 baby chicks. Curious, the hatchery man asked why the Norwegian came in every week to order 200 more chicks.
"Vell," said the Norwegian. "Something seems to be wrong . . . eeder I'm planting dem too deep . . . or too close together."

161

How can Swedes distinguish boy sardines
from girl sardines?
They watch to see which can they come out of.

■   ■   ■   ■

Why don't Swedes watch the Gong Show?
It's too intellectual.

■   ■   ■   ■

A Swede had been out "on the town" and after too many
drinks staggered into the barn to sleep it off. Unknow-
ingly, he settled in with some pigs. When he awoke next
morning, he felt a warm body near his back, so he gave a
nudge with his elbow, asking, "Er du Svensk?"
Answered the pig: "Norsk . . . Norsk."

■   ■   ■   ■

A Norwegian was hired to paint the center stripe down
the middle of a new highway. The first day he completed
3 miles, two miles the second day, but only one the 3rd
day. Noting the difference, the superintendent asked for
an explanation.
"I dunno," puzzled the Norwegian, "I guess it just kept
getting farther to go back to that can of paint."

"THE LEFSE SONG"
(May be sung to the tune of "Camptown Races")

Norsky ladies sing dis song . . . Uff Da! Uff Da.
Bake dat lefse all day long . . . all da Uff Da day.
Bake it till it's almost brown . . . Uff Da! Uff Da
Makes you yump yust like a clown . . .
all da Uff Da Day.

(CHORUS)

Gonna bake all night . . . gonna bake all day
I'll spend my money on potatoes and flour . . .
To have me an Uff Da day.

Vent down town for some lutefisk . . . Uff da! Uff Da!
De vedder vas so cold and brisk, all da Uff Da day.
Used my lefse for a Mackinaw . . . Uff Da . . . Uff Da
Greatest yacket I ever saw . . .
Lefse saved da day.

(CHORUS)

Vent to town in my model T . . . Uff Da . . . Uff Da.
Tire vent flat and I said "Poor Me." . . .
it vas an Uff Da day
Used dat lefse for a patch . . . Uff Da . . . Uff Da!
Now I gotta bake me anodder batch . . .
Oh da Uff da day.

(CHORUS)

Last vinter I lost my undervear . . . Uff Da! Uff Da!
But dis Norvegian didn't care . . .
all da Uff Da day.
Sewed some lefse into BVD's . . . Uff Da . . . Uff Da.
Fixed me up so I didn't freeze . . .
all da Uff Da day.

(CHORUS)

Ven day ask me how I spell "relief" . . . Uff Da . . . Uff Da
I tell dem lefse saves me grief,
any Uff Da day
Don't need Rolaids or Di-Yell . . . Uff Da Uff Da
Yust give me lefse and I'll get well,
any old Uff Da day.
(FINAL CHORUS)

■   ■   ■   ■

SWEDE: When is your birthday?
NORWEGIAN: March 21st.
SWEDE: What year?
NORWEGIAN: Every year.

■   ■   ■   ■

JUDGE: You've been brought here for drinking.
DANE: Swell! Let's get started.

164

"Little Norwegian House on the Prairie"

HILDA: Vhen ve vere younger, Lars,
you used to nibble on my ear.
(Lars starts to leave the room)
HILDA: Vhere are you going, Lars?
LARS: Into da bedroom to get my teeth.

"AY VANT TO GO BAKK"

(May be sung to the tune of "My Little Grass Shack"

Oh . . . ay vant to go bakk
To dat liddle tar paper shakk . . .
In Du-loota Minne-soota
Vhere da Norskies and da Svenskies
vatch da Lutefisk go svimming by.

I can hear Ole Olson singing
In da garden of St. Paul.
I can hear yust vhat he's singing . . .
(Audience: "Vhat?")
Sild og potato . . . rolle polse . . .
knakke brod . . . og ost

Oh ay vant to go bakk
To dat liddle tar paper shakk . . .
In Du-loota Minnes-soota
Vhere da Norskies and da Svenskies
vatch da Lutefisk go svimming by!

■ ■ ■ ■

TENA: "Ven are you getting married, Lena?"
LENA: "I'm in no hurry . . . dere is plenty of fish
in da ocean."
TENA: "Yah, dat's right, but your bait
is getting stale."

Why does it take three Swedes to eat a rabbit?
Because it requires two just to look out for cars.

. . . .

A Dane stopped a taxicab in Chicago and asked the driver,
"Do you have room for a six pack of beer and a pizza?"
"Yeh, buddy, sure do," said the Cabby.
So the Dane threw up in the back seat.

. . . .

COACH: Ole, we're short on players.
Do you think you can pass this football?"
OLE: "Yah, Coach, I tink I can if I can svallow it."

. . . .

Did you hear about the 900 Norwegians
that committed suicide?
They were trying to keep up with the Joneses.

. . . .

MARRIAGE COUNSELOR: You say you are having
marital problems. Do you have mutual climax?
NORWEGIAN: No . . . our insurance is
Lut'ran Brudderhood.

OLE HAD HIS HEART SET
ON WIRE FRAMES.

FIVE

more UFF DA JOKES

A Norwegian went to an eye doctor to have his eyes checked for glasses. The doctor directed him to read various letters with the left eye while covering the right eye. The Norwegian was so mixed up on which eye was which that the eye doctor in disgust took a paper sack with a hole to see through, covered up the appropriate eyes and asked the Norwegian to read the letters. As he did so, he noticed the Norwegian had tears streaming down his face. "Look," said the doctor, "there's no need to get emotional about getting glasses."
"I know," agreed the Norwegian, "But I kind of had my heart set on vire frames."

. . . .

Torkelson was given a bottle of medicine for his hearing problem. It must have worked, because two days later he heard from his uncle in Norway.

A Norwegian in our town is so dumb that he thinks "decaffeinated" refers to a cow that has just given birth.

. . . .

A Norwegian and a Swede were discussing the great wonders of the world.

"Vell, I tink da greatest tings on earth are da Grand Canyon and da Empire State building," said the Swede.

"Oh, dey're purty good . . . but for my money, da Termos jug is da most amazing and vunderful ting on earth. Why it keeps cold tings cold and hot tings hot," said the Norwegian.

"Well, what's so amazing about THAT?" exclaimed the Swede.

"Becoss," said the Norwegian, "I can't help vondering, HOW DO IT KNOW?"

. . . .

WIFE: Well, dear, how was the fishing trip?
DANE: (who had done a lot more than fish) Oh, fine . . . great in fact. We caught quite a few but we gave 'em all to the guides.
But, you know something? You forgot to pack my toothbrush and shaving kit."
WIFE: "I put them," she said icily, "in your tackle box."

Norwegian Snow Blower

A recent earthquake in California was caused, we hear, when they tried to bury a Norwegian. The earth rejected the body.

. . . .

Ole went into the fertilizer business and became rather successful.

"In fact," he told Blomquist, "I guess you could say ve are number vun in number two."

A telephone company hired a bunch of Scandinavians to put in a new line of telephone poles in an area they had contracted to serve. They hired mostly Swedes and Norwegians. After the first day, the foreman came around to check with the Norwegians. He said, "The Swedes put in 46 poles today. How many did you Norwegians put in?"

"Vell, ve put in two," answered one of the Norwegians.

"ONLY TWO?" exclaimed the foreman. "Why, the Swedes put in 46!"

"Yah, dat's right," said the Norwegian, "But for gosh sakes, did you notice how much dey left sticking out of da ground?"

. . . .

Up in Northern Norway, near Spitzbergen, lies a strip of land between Russia and Norway. One particular land parcel had gone back and forth between Russia and Norway for a period of a hundred years. Finally, the spot where Ole the Norwegian lived was turned back to Norway.

"Thank goodness," commented Ole. "I don't think I could stand any more Russian vinters."

. . . .

Why do Norwegians make the worst sky divers?
—Because they keep missing the earth.

172

Helga was a spinster who, although rather plain, had an eye for the young men of her town. One night she cornered young Leif at the dance.

"Leif," she said, "it vould be so nice if you vould valk me to my house. I yust LOVE having experienced men take me home."

"But," protested Leif, "I'M not experienced."

"No," agreed Helga, "but ve're not home YET!"

∎　∎　∎　∎

A Swede was sentenced to be executed,
so the warden asked what he wanted
for his last meal.
"Strawberries," answered the Swede.
"STRAWBERRIES?" exclaimed the warden.
"Strawberries won't be in season
for a least four months."
"I can wait," said the Swede.

∎　∎　∎　∎

JENS: Say, Karl . . . I haven't seen you in years . . . you used to be skinny and now you're fat. You used to have a lot of hair and now you're bald. You used to be tall and now you're short.
STRANGER: My name ain't Karl . . . it's Robin Williams.
JENS: Oh! So you changed your name too!

Norwegian Peeping Tom

An old Norwegian sea captain operating out of New York had a ritual each morning while at sea. The First Mate would observe the Captain going to a wall safe, taking out a piece of paper, examining it briefly, then putting it back and locking the safe. After 20 years of this, the first mate's curiosity was stimulated. Finally, the old Captain died. Taking over the Captain's duties, the First Mate's first move was to force open the safe in the wall. Sure enough, there was a box and in it the paper. The First Mate read these words on the paper: "Port . . . Left. Starboard, Right."

■ ■ ■ ■

Ole was telling Toivo, "I yust got a set of dem Italian tires. Dey go "WOP, WOP, WOP, WOP."

■ ■ ■ ■

Helga, the Swedish Spinster, called the police: "Dere is a prowler in my house; vould you come by in the morning and pick him up?"

■ ■ ■ ■

A Swede, it seems, got Herpes of the eyes.
He'd been "looking for love
in all the wrong places."

175

INGRID: I voke last night and vas shivering all over.
LENA: Did your teeth chatter?
INGRID: I don't know . . .
we haven't slept togedder for years.

•   •   •   •

A Swede traveled across the United States to Yellowstone Park. When he saw a sign "Bear Left," he got disgusted and went back home.

•   •   •   •

Did you hear about the Norwegian who was so simple that:
—He thought Ernest Tubb was a sincere place to bathe.
—He thought Johnny Cash was money for a pay toilet.
—He thought Slim Whitman was a thin box of chocolates.
—He called his girl friend "Hershey" because she was half nuts.
—He closed his eyes in Sears when he saw a sign, "Women's Bloomers—half Off".
—He thought Gerald Ford was a car agency.
—He thought Taco Bell was a Mexican telephone company.
—He thought "goblets" were small sailors.

A Norwegian who had a very heavy accent was trying to learn to talk like other Americans where he was living in Minnesota. Seems that everywhere he went, people spotted him as a Norwegian because of his accent. So, the Norwegian spent $500 on diction lessons, hoping to sound like an average American.

After his final lesson, the Norwegian decided to try out his new diction by going shopping. He went into a store and approached a clerk.

"I would like to buy . . . a pound of butter . . . a dozen eggs, two pounds of hamburger, and a ring of baloney," said the Norwegian.

"You're Norwegian, aren't you?" asked the clerk.

"Yes, I am," answered the surprised Norwegian. "How could you tell?"

"Because, you're in a Hardware store," responded the clerk.

■ ■ ■ ■

TEACHER: Swen, what does RFD stand for?
SWEDISH KID: Ranklin Felano Doosevelt.

■ ■ ■ ■

Ole says: "I never knew vhat happiness vas until I got married. By dat time, it vas too late."

What is the best way to get the attention
of a Swede?
—Simply call out:
"ATTENTION K MART SHOPPERS!"

■ ■ ■ ■

A minister named Adams was preparing his Sunday sermon and told his wife Dianne he was going to talk about
skiing. The wife had a cold on Sunday and didn't go to
church. The minister absent mindedly forgot to tell his
wife that he changed his sermon to talk about SEX. So the
next day, when a lady from the congregation met the minister's wife on the street, she said how interesting the
minister's sermon was on Sunday.
"Oh, I really didn't think he should have chosen that
topic," said the minister's wife; "He has only tried it
twice, and he fell off both times."

■ ■ ■ ■

A Swede went on his first airplane flight. After being
strapped in and getting adjusted to his new surroundings,
the Swede got up his nerve to look out the window. "Yee
Vhiz," he exclaimed. "Ve must be up high . . .
da people down dere all look like ants."
"Those ARE ants," explained the stewardess.
"We're not off the ground yet."

178

(Tree Below Zero)

Norwegian Weather Report

A fairly handsome Swede walked into a drug store in North Dakota one day where he encountered a lady clerk.

—"Do you have a man clerk?" he inquired nervously.

—"No," answered the lady, "my sister and I are the only ones working here. But, we own the store and we've heard EVERYTHING in the way of problems, so feel free to ask me anything."

—"Well," said the Swede, "I have this problem where I have to have sex three or four times a day. What can you do for me?"

—The lady clerk disappeared in the back room to talk to her sister. Five minutes later she reappeared.

—"I talked it over with my sister, and the best we can do for you is $1,000 a month and half interest in the store!"

Swenson was a Swedish farmer with an attractive young wife whom he suspected of cheating on him a few times. Since his livestock business took him away from home sometimes for a week or more, he would check up on his wife occasionally by telephone.

One day he called and the phone was answered by a strange voice. "Who is this?" asked Swenson.

"Dis is Tina, da new hired girl."

"Vell, let me speak to my vife," said Swenson.

"She's in bed . . . vith some man," answered Tina. Swenson exploded on the other end of the line.

"Tina," he said, "this is the last straw. I want you to go in the kitchen cupboard . . . one of the drawers has a gun. I vant you to go in the bedroom and shoot both of dem."

"I couldn't do dat," protested Tina.

"Vell, I'll give you $5,000 if you do," responded Swenson. Tina thought for a minute and finally said, "All right, Sir. I sure could use da money. Yust vait a little." Swenson waited and listened and shortly he heard two shots. A couple of minutes later, Tina was back on the line. "Vell, I did it, Sir. Vhat should I do vit da bodies?"

"Oh," said Swenson, "yust drag 'em to da vell outside the back porch and toss 'em in."

"But dere isn't any vell," protested Tina.

"NO WELL?" exploded Swenson. "Isn't dis 356-9087?"

■ ■ ■ ■

Sven lives in such a small town that the 7-11 is called "3½-5½".

180

KARL: Ole, vhen did you start vearing a girdle?
OLE: Da same day my vife found vun in my glove compartment.

■　■　■　■

A Norwegian named Carl Norlander was a real estate man. After selling a house to a Swedish couple, Norlander received a call from the lady who had bought the house. She explained that her husband was on the road, working, and that since she had found a fault with the house, she wanted the money back immediately without waiting for her husband's return. The problem, she explained, was that the house was so close to the railroad, that every time the train went by, it shook her out of bed since she slept in the nude between satin sheets. The realtor drove over to check the story, and since a train was due in a few minutes, he took off all his clothes to see if he would, in fact, be vibrated out of bed. As he lay there, the woman's husband unexpectedly walked in the house, noted Norlander in the bed, and ripped off the top sheet. Seeing the realtor in the "altogether" he angrily shouted, "What is the meaning of this?"

"Would you believe," asked the realtor meekly, "that I'm waiting for a train?"

■　■　■　■

A Norwegian kid wanted a watch for Christmas
—So, at Christmas, his folks let him.

Ole and Lena, who had recently been married, were driving along the road when Lena began feeling amorous.

"Ole, let's stop da car and have ourselves a good time," suggested Lena.

"How in da vorld could ve do dat?" exclaimed Ole. Ve're out in public. Everybody vould see us."

"Vell, dat's no problem," answered Lena. "Ve can yust get under da car."

"yah, but vhat if somebody comes by and says sumting?" Ole commented.

"Vell, in case somebody stops and asks vhat you are doing, yust say you're fixing da clutch."

So, Lena finally convinced Ole, and they stopped the car and got under it. As they were commencing to have a good time, Lars Olson walked by and said, "Ole, vhat in da vorld are you doing?"

"Can't you see I'm under here fixing da clutch?" said Ole.

"Vell," responded Lars. "You better vork on da brakes first . . . da car has rolled half a block down da street."

■   ■   ■   ■

An elderly Norwegian got out of his easy chair to answer the doorbell. There at the door stood a voluptuous gorgeous young woman.

—"Oh Dear," she exclaimed. "I'm at the wrong house."

—"You're at the right house," said the old Norwegian "but you're 40 years too late."

182

HOW TO MAKE A NORWEGIAN DIME'ND PIN

FIRST GET A SAFETY PIN

THEN FIND A DIME

TURN DIME OVER "HEADS DOWN" LEAVING "TAILS" LOOKING AT YOU

POSITION PIN ON TOP OF DIME AS IN ILLUSTRATION

HOLD HOT SOLDERING IRON ON SPOT INDICATED UNTIL SOLDER MELTS AND SPREADS OUT. LET COOL AND YOU HAVE A GENUINE NORWEGIAN DIME'ND PIN

Bruce Johnson, an eye doctor from Casper, Wyoming, made a spectacle of himself by sending us this gem:

A Norwegian lad named Lars, who hailed from Grand Forks, N. Dak., received a scholarship to go to Yale. The neighbors were all surprised when he came back home before the school year ended.

Lars explained, "Vell, I vasn't doing too bad in the books, but I vas ashamed of myself dat I couldn' learn da vords to da school fight song:

    Boola boola, boola boola, boola boola, boola boo.
    Boola boola, boola boola, boola boola, boola boo.

It vas yust too complicated, so I decided to qvit school and come back to Nort Dakota."

■ ■ ■ ■

An old Irish lady approached a Norwegian visiting in Ireland, asking if he would locate her son, John Dunne, who had left for America and hadn't written as promised. When the Norwegian reached New York, he spied a sign, "Dun & Bradstreet."

Certain that he'd found his man, the Norwegian walked in asked if they had a "John."

"Yes, down the hall," answered the secretary. The Norwegian walked into the restroom and saw a man standing at a urinal. "Are you Dunne?" asked the Norwegian.

"Yes, I'm done," said the man.

"Vell," said the Norwegian, "Why don't you write to your poor mudder in Ireland?"

184

Ole the Norwegian and noted poet Robert Frost both died the same day. Since things were crowded at the Pearly Gates at the time, St. Peter told the two that only one could be admitted. So, he told Ole and Robert Frost to each write a poem using the word "Timbuktu."

Frost, being a professional, finished his poem first and presented it to St. Peter. It read:

"While travelling in a distant land,
My feet upon the burning sand
I saw a train a-passing through
On the way to Timbuktu

St. Peter was very impressed, but felt that to be fair they should also consider Ole's poem, which was as follows:

Old Tim and I a hunting went
Spied some maidens in a tent
They were three and we were two
I bucked one and Timbuktu!

■　■　■　■

Bjarne started off for home, and being late, decided to go through the woods. Being a bit nervous about the possibility of meeting a bear, he asked Lars what he should do if he met one.

"Vell," said Lars, all you have to do is run like hell and if da bear gets too close, turn around grab a handful and throw it in da bear's face."

Said Bjarne, "A handful of WHAT?"

Lars: Don't worry . . . it'll be there.

A Swede tried unsuccessfully for months to collect a bill from a Dane. He finally sent a sob story to the debtor along with a picture of his little daughter. Under it he wrote, "This is why I need the money."

By return mail the Dane sent a picture of a beautiful girl in a bikini with the message, "This is why I can't pay."

▪ ▪ ▪ ▪

Two Norwegians were walking down the street in St. Paul when they encountered a neighborhood priest with his arm in a cast.

"Vhat happened to your arm, Fadder?" asked one of the Norwegians.

"I slipped in the bathtub and broke it."

Later, one Norwegian asked the other, "Vhat is a bath tub?"

"How should I know," retorted the other.

"I'm not Catlick."

▪ ▪ ▪ ▪

A Swedish lady, Aleen Colvin, who had just given birth to triplets, was explaining to a neighbor that "it happens only once every 20,000 times."

"Goodness sakes," exclaimed the neighbor,

"How did you ever get time to do your housevork?"

Ludwig made a visit to the church on the corner near his home, found a priest and proceeded to make a confession.

"Father, I got some tings to tell you about. I had an affair vid da vidow on Oak Street last veek.

And dis veek I been getting togedder vid a coupla married vomen in my apartment."

"Well," said the priest, "for penance you'd better go home and say 40 Hail Marys."

"Oh, I ain't Cat'lick," explained Ludwig.

"You're not CATHOLIC?" exclaimed the priest. "Then, why are you telling ME?"

"Becoss," said Ludwig, "I'm telling EVERYBODY!"

■　■　■　■

A Swede was sympathizing with a Norwegian who had lost three wives in less than a year. The Swede asked how they died.

"Vell, da first vun died from poisoned mushrooms," explained the Norwegian.

"And the second one?" asked the Swede?

"Same ting . . . poisoned mushrooms."

"How about the last one," asked the puzzled Swede.

"Oh her," said the Norwegian, "Fractured Skull."

"How come?"

"Wouldn't eat her mushrooms."

A California court recently had an interesting case involving a Norwegian. The District Attorney, Bee Donaghue had the case pretty well wrapped up. So, the Norwegian's attorney, Bob Ward said to the Norwegian, "Here's my suggestion, Ole. I'm going to plead for clemency."
"Nuttin' doing," exclaimed the Norwegian,
"Let Clemency hire his own lawyer."

NORWEGIAN SNOW TIRE
MADE OF 100% PURE SNOW

Did you hear about the Norwegian mosquito?
—He bit Dolly Parton on the ANKLE.

.   .   .   .

SVEN: I have the best hearing aid on the market.
Cost me $3,000.
NELS: Vhat kind is it?
SVEN: Five O'Clock.

.   .   .   .

Ole and Lars were crazy about baseball. They even spec-
ulated on the possibility of baseball being played in
heaven. So they made an agreement . . . whoever went
first would find a way to tell the other back on earth
whether or not baseball was played in heaven.
Lars was the first to go, and one day as Ole was walking
down the street, he felt a slight tap on his shoulder.
"Is dat you, Lars?" asked Ole.
"Yah, it's me, Ole. I've got some good news and some
bad news."
"Vell," said Ole, "let's have da good news first."
"Da good news, Ole," said Lars, "is dat YES, dere is baseball in heaven."
"OK," responded Ole. "Now what is da bad news?"
Answered Lars, "You're scheduled to pitch next Tues-
day."

JOHAN: I finally got your sister to say yes.
NELS: Svell. Good News. Ven is da vedding?
JOHAN: What vedding?

. . . .

Back in the barnstorming days, airplane pilots gave rides in open cockpit planes. One day Nels Simons, a farmer from near Renner, S.D., got curious about going up in a plane.

The pilot said he would take Simons and his wife up for $4, but if they could keep quiet during the flight, they could go for $2. Simons agreed. The pilot, not wanting to lose the extra two dollars, really put the plane into all sorts of maneuvers . . . barrel rolls, loop the loops, and to finish off, flew upside down for five minutes. As he landed the plane, he remarked to Simons, "You are bravest man I ever took up. You didn't say one word." The farmer said, "Vell, I came purty close to saying sumting ven my vife fell out."

. . . .

We recently heard about a Dane who had to stay home one day because of illness. That day he found out how very much his wife loved him. She was SO excited. Every time the mailman or a delivery man arrived, she would shout loudly, "MY HUSBAND'S HOME! MY HUSBAND'S HOME!"

LUTEFISK IN DA VINDOW

How much is dat lutefisk in da vindow?
Da vun vid da baby blue eyes.
How much is dat lutefisk in da vindow?
I tink it should vin a virst prize

I heard on da radio dere's a special,
On Lutefisk . . . ten cents a pound.
I ran clear down town so I could buy some,
But now dey have took da sign down.

How much is dat lutefisk in da vindow?
Vid lefse it sure vill taste fine.
I'll smear on some butter to improve it,
If only dat Lutefisk was mine.

I don't vant no pork chops or a T bone.
I don't vant no hot dog on a bun.
I must have my lutefisk and lefse,
Cause dat's how a Norsky has fun.

How much is dat Lutefisk in da vindow?
Da vun vid da baby blue eyes.
I vant to take it home instead of herring,
And give my vife qvite a surprise.

■　■　■　■

Why don't Swedes eat M & M's?
Because they're too hard to peel.

191

A Swede in our town was never able to develop a liking for Norwegians. So, one of his fellow Swedes was surprised one day to see the Swede give a coin to a monkey perched on the instrument of a Norwegian organ grinder. "I thought you didn't like Norwegians," said the friend. "Yah, dat's true," replied the Swede. "But they are so cute when dey are little."

■　■　■　■

Three couples were being considered for membership in the Trinity Church. The minister explained that one of the requirements was for the couple to abstain from relations three weeks prior to final approval. "When you demonstrate self control, you will be welcomed to membership in the Trinity Church," explained the minister.

Two of the couples indicated compliance, so the minister said, "You are now welcomed to membership in the Trinity Church.

However, the Norwegian and his wife admitted that on the last day of the three week period, they had succumbed after the Norwegian became aroused when his wife leaned over to pick up a spool of thread that had dropped on the floor.

"I'm extremely sorry," said the minister, "but I have to say that you now cannot be welcomed into the Trinity Church."

"Vell," said the Norwegian, "ve are not velcome at Sears and Roebuck anymore eeder."

HOW TO MAKE A NORWEGIAN FLY SWATTER

NORWEGIAN FLY SWATTER

GET A STICK 12" LONG 3/4" WIDE

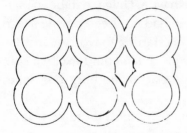

HAVE SOMEONE
DRINK A 6-PAK
OF BEER OR POP
KEEP THE PLASTIC PART

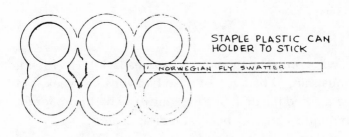

STAPLE PLASTIC CAN
HOLDER TO STICK

NORWEGIAN FLY SWATTER

193

Knute Knutson had worked hard and finally accumulated enough money to move into town. So he ordered a fine large house to be constructed. "And," he told the contractor, "I vant you should put a 'halo statue' in every room." "What in the world is a 'halo statue'?" inquired the contractor. "Vell, you know, dat's vun of dem gadgets you put in da house, and the bell rings and you run over and pick it up and say, 'halo, Statue'?"

．　．　．　．

Swen Carlson and his Swedish wife, Helga, had been married for 15 years. Lately, Swen had not been paying much attention to Helga and she was starting to worry. One day she read in a magazine how a woman could excite a man by greeting him at the door clad in nothing but Saran Wrap.
So, when Swen arrived home that night, there was Helga at the door . . . nothing on but Saran Wrap.
Swen snorted, "Hah! Left overs again!"

．　．　．　．

Axel was complaining about a bad headache. His friend, Rasmus said, "I had vun of dose bad vuns last veek, but my vife cured me of it. She took me in da bedroom for fifteen minutes and my headache disappeared."
Axel reached for his hat and coat and said, "Vell, I've tried everything else . . . is your vife home NOW?"

NORSKY FROM MINN'OPLIS

Norskies don't smoke no pot in Minneapolis
A place vere even Svedes can have a ball
Ve fill up on lutefisk and lefse
And snoose is da biggest treat of all.

Ve don't make no trouble vid da Irish
And da Polish people say ve're number vun
Ve let da Viking team fight all our battles
Vile ve take part in all da tailgate fun

I'm proud to be a Norsky from Minneapolis
A place where even Svedes can do their ting
Drinking beer and smoking ol' Bull Durham
And vatching how dat Hennepin can sving.

Dat Bud Grant feller may not be a Norsky
But he's a reg'lar viking yust the same
He took a bunch of rookies to da stadium
And teached dem how to play dat football game.

And I'm proud to be a Norsky from Minneapolis
A place where even Svedes can get along
Vunce a munth we go to Sons of Norvay
An' ve say "Uff Da" ven da Tvins go wrong.

Vunce a munth ve go to Sons of Norvay
In Minnoplis, Minnesota, U.S.A.

We had a Norwegian lawyer in our town
who spent all night with a widow
trying to break her will.

■　■　■　■

A Danish couple decided to get a divorce because of incompatability.
He's lost his income, and she had lost her pat-ability.

■　■　■　■

A Norwegian brought his little yellow dog into a bar and ordered a beer. Big Swen, a burly Swede, was also standing at the bar with his large black dog at his feet. Big Swen, who was a bit of a bully, goaded the Norwegian into an argument about whose dog was toughest. The Norwegian was reluctant but finally the Swede issued a challenge to see which dog could whip the other.
Finally, the Swede seized the initiative and "sicced" his big black dog on the Norwegian's little yellow dog. Two minutes later, there was nothing but a pile of fur left on the floor . . . the little yellow dog had torn the black dog to pieces! The astonished crowd gathered around and asked the Norwegian where in the world he got that amazing yellow dog.
"Vell," said the Norwegian, "before I trimmed off some of his nose and painted him yellow, he vas an alligator."

MOTTO FOUND IN
OLE'S REC ROOM.

Norwegian Weather Report: Dark tonight;
possibly sunny tomorrow.

■　■　■　■

When Ole was courting Lena, they spent the day at the
beach, watching the ocean roll in. In a poetic mood, Ole
waxed eloquent: "Roll on, thou wild and restless ocean!
Roll on!"
—After a brief pause, Lena looked adoringly at Ole and
said, "Oh Ole! It's DOING it!"

Everyone who reads those weekly "scandal sheets" has noticed those "lonely hearts" ads from all over the country. A Norwegian farmer in North Dakota recently placed the following ad:
"Honest, sincere North Dakota farmer, Norwegian, seeks correspondence with husky and healthy lady with tractor. Please send picture of tractor."

■   ■   ■   ■

A Finn tried to learn to be a carpenter, but he had the misfortune of burning down the house he was building when he tried to weld two 2X4's together.

■   ■   ■   ■

KNUTE: My second cousin yust von a million dollars in da New York lottery.
He says he's never going to vork anudder day in his life?
NELS: Oh, he's quitting his yob?
KNUTE: No, he's staying on at da post office.

■   ■   ■   ■

A Norwegian flasher announced he was planning to retire. But his friends talked him into sticking it out for another year.

A Finn in our town circled the block 58 times recently . . . his turn signal had gotten stuck.

. . . .

Why did the Lord give Denmark such a beautiful land with so much good soil, while He gave Norway such rocky land hardly fit for farming? Explanation: Because he messed up so bad on the Danes' language.

. . . .

Lena was happily married to Carl and they had 5 children. Then Carl died. Shortly, Lena married Sven, and they had 4 children. Then, Sven died. Before long, Lena married Ole and they had 5 children. Then Ole died. Then, it wasn't long before Lena died.

At the funeral, friends filed past the casket. One lady murmured, "See how nice she looks, and isn't it nice they are together again."

The lady behind her asked, "Who do you mean? Lena and Carl?"

"No," said the lady.

"Vell den, you mean Lena and Sven?"

"No," answered the lady.

"Den, you must mean Lena and Ole?"

"No," said the lady. "I mean her knees."

The Seattle city government was making an effort to bring minority groups, such as Norwegians, into their work force. So, they interviewed a token Norwegian and gave him some word tests. He had a difficult time spelling, so the examiner decided to give him a real simple word.

"Spell DOG," said the examiner.

"D-d-d-d-" the Norwegian stammered in puzzlement.

"Come on, you can do it," encouraged the examiner.

In frustration the Norwegian pounded his head and muttered, "Oh gee!"

"That's right," exclaimed the employment examiner. "You're hired!"

■　■　■　■

DANE: I better go home . . . my wife is in bed with Laryngitis.

NORWEGIAN: Is dat Greek back in town again?

■　■　■　■

Lars had the misfortune of being bit by a rodent. A couple of days later, the doctor came over and told Lars he was afraid he might have rabies. Lars immediately sat down at the table and started writing. "What are you doing, Lars? Making out your will?" asked the doctor.

"No," answered Lars. "I'm making a list of people I'm gonna bite."

LARS: Vhy did you leave Helga's house so early
last night?
SVEN: Vell, she took me in da parlor and started
kissing me and hugging me, and everyting vas vonderful.
Den, all of a sudden, she reached up and turned
off da light. Vell, I took da hint and vent home.

■   ■   ■   ■

"Papa," said little Hjalmar, "Vhy did you sign my report
card vid an X instead of signing your name?
Papa Lars replied, "I sure didn't vant your teacher to tink
anyvun vid your grades could have a fadder who could
read and write."

■   ■   ■   ■

Ole and Lena were out motoring one day in Ole's new
car. A policeman stopped him and said he was doing 50
miles per hour in a 30 mile zone.
"I vas only going 30, officer", protested Ole.
"No, you were going 50," said the cop.
"Really, officer, I vas yust doing 30," said Ole.
"And I say you were going 50," repeated the cop.
Lena, sitting in the back seat, trying to be helpful, spoke
up,
"Officer . . . you shouldn't try to argue vid Ole ven he's
been drinking!"

OLE (on the telephone): Hurry, get an ambulance over here, my vife is going to have a baby!
NURSE: Calm down, sir. Is this her first baby?
OLE: No . . . this is her husband.

. . . .

Did you hear how the Norwegian hockey team drowned?
—They were trying to practice during the summer.

. . . .

A Norwegian was witnessing his first jet plane . . . flying at 20,000 feet and leaving a vapor trail.
"Yeepers Creepers," he exclaimed,
"Look how high dat crop duster is flying!"

. . . .

A Norwegian lady named Ingeborg met her Swedish friend, Helga, after several years. Ingeborg explained that she had been married four times. First, to a banker, who died. Then, to a theater owner; and he died also. The third husband was a preacher, who met an untimely end; and her fourth husband was an undertaker. Ingeborg explained: "Yah, it's kinda funny vit my husbands . . .
it vas vun for da money, two for da show,
three to get ready, and four to go."

THREE POSITIONS for NORWEGIAN HEADWEAR

1 OFF

2 ON

3 LOCK

A Norwegian accidentally dropped his jacket into an outhouse. He was making quite a fuss so his companion commented, "Why don't you forget it . . . it's an old jacket anyway."

"I know it," said the Norwegian, "but I got my lunch in the pocket."

■ ■ ■ ■

Jensen, the Dane, was experiencing fading health so he went to a doctor. "Your hearing is getting terrible," said the doctor, "and you've got to give up smoking, drinking and chasing women."

"Ridiculous!" exclaimed Jensen. "Give up all that just so I can hear a little better?"

■ ■ ■ ■

The U.S. Army recently recruited a number of women from Wisconsin. As they were being processed, they were asked how many pairs of underwear they required.

"Seven," said the German girl.

"One for each day of the week."

The Irish girl asked for four:

"One for each week in the month."

The Norwegian girl asked for twelve.

"How come so many?" asked the puzzled sergeant.

"Vell," explained the Norwegian girl, "Vun for Yanuary, vun for February, . . . etc."

What do you get when you cross a Norwegian with a pig?
—Nothing. There are some things even a pig won't do.

．　．　．　．

A Swede got loaded one night and wandered into a subway in New York. After he finally found his way out, he met up with his buddy who asked where he had been. The Swede replied, "Vell, I vent down some steps and ended up in some guy's basement . . . and boy! You should see da electric train set he's got down dere!"

．　．　．　．

Two Norwegian brothers named Simons were business partners. One day they decided to hire a new secretary. Gordon had to go on a trip to Chicago, so he left it up to brother John to place an ad and to interview any applicants. A few days later, Gordon called on the phone to inquire about the secretary.

"Well," said John, "three ladies came in. I asked the first one, "How much is two and two," and she said 'four.' I asked the second one how much is two and two, and she said 'five.' So I asked the third one 'how much is two and two,' and she says, "How much do you want it to be?"

"Well," said Gordon on the phone, "Which one did you hire?"

Answered John, "The one with the big bosoms."

INQUIRING REPORTER: What do you think
of the Indianapolis 500?
NORWEGIAN: Vell, I tink dey're all guilty

■　■　■　■

SAME INQUIRING REPORTER: What do you think
of Red China?
DANE: If you have a yellow table cloth,
it should look all right.

■　■　■　■

Describe Danish cough medicine:
A bottle of Castor oil. Two spoonfuls
and you don't DARE cough.

■　■　■　■

An ocean going liner was sailing the Atlantic when it hit an
iceberg. Survivors were able to take to lifeboats except
one boat that was overloaded by three persons. Nobly, a
Frenchman volunteered to sacrifice himself, leaping in
the water with a shout, "Vive La France." Next, and
Englishman stepped to the edge of the boat, bravely calling out, "God Save the Queen," then jumped into the
ocean.
Finally, a Norwegian stood up, reached over and grabbed
a Swede. He shoved the Swede into the water, and then
shouted out, "Long live Norway."

What is the most frequently heard remark
in a Norwegian operating room?
—"Oops!"

. . . .

Ole walked into a neighborhood bar and proclaimed in a
voice everyone could hear:
"Ven Ole drinks, EVERYBODY drinks!"
Whereupon everyone in the crowded bar rushed up to
order themselves a drink. As Ole finished his drink and
wiped off his mouth and chin, he announced as he
walked to the door:
"And when Ole pays, EVERYBODY pays!"

. . . .

The evangelist was preaching hell, fire and brimstone
when he shouted, "If any man among us thinks he is perfect, let him stand up."
Torkelson in the front row stood up.
"And you think you're perfect?" thundered the
evangelist.
"No sir, not me," came the reply. "I'm standing up for my
wife's first husband."

. . . .

A Swede had the silly notion that a Pap test was a blood
check to see who the father is.

SIX

OLE & LENA JOKES

Ole, Lars and Knute were discussing ferocious creatures.
Lars said, "Da tiger-eating alligator has got to be da meanest animal alive."

Knute held another opinion, saying, "Vell, I tink dat da alligator eating tiger is really da meanest of any animal anywhere."

Ole spoke up, saying, "I hate to disagree, but in my opinion, da Tigergator is da meanest critter you'll find anywhere."

"Da Tigergator?" exclaimed Lars and Knute in a chorus. What in da vorld is a Tigergator?"

Replied Ole, "Da Tigergator has a tiger's head on one end and an alligator's head on the other."

"But . . . how does he go to the bathroom?" asked Lars.

"He doesn't," said Ole. "Dat's vhat makes him so mean."

Ole had a mishap while working on a roofing job. He slid off the roof . . . and came down with the shingles.
"Fortunately," said Ole, "I vas vearing my light Fall suit."

■ ■ ■ ■

OLE: Vhy do you suppose Norvegians don't vear tennis shoes?
SWEDE: I tink it's becoss seed corn companies don't give dem away.

■ ■ ■ ■

Ole called the doctor and asked him to come over and have a look at his son-in-law who had buckshot in his rear quarters. The doctor queried, "Why in the world would you fire buckshot at your son-in-law?"
To which Ole replied, "Vhen I fired da buckshot, he vasn't my son in law."

■ ■ ■ ■

Ole caught a ride from Fargo to Chicago. The truck driver let him off on North Michigan Avenue. Ole was trying to catch a cab to take him downtown. A cab came along and Ole hollered, "DO YOU GO TO DA LOOP?"
"No," replied the cab driver. "I go BEEP BEEP."

Ole came home one night somewhat intoxicated. Acting a bit feisty, Ole said to Lena, "Lena, you remind me of a John Deere tractor." Lena chose to ignore him and went about fixing Ole's supper for him. A bit later, Ole said, "Lena, on second thought, you remind me of a Massey-Ferguson combine." Again, Lena ignored the remark since Ole was always a bit argumentative after drinking. But the supper mellowed Ole up somewhat, and by bed time, he was in a very good mood. In fact, after turning out the lights, Ole said, "Lena, how about you and me having some fun?"

"Ole," said Lena, "If you tink I'm going to start up dis 85 tousand dollar combine for yust a half an ear of corn, YOU'RE CRASY!"

■　■　■　■

When Ole and Lena moved to a larger city, Little Ole was enrolled in a school in a mixed neighborhood. One day, when he came home from school, he asked, "If Jesus vas a Jew, how come he had a Puerto Rican name?"

■　■　■　■

Ole went to the store and bought a can of Beethoven brand beans . . . because Lena enjoys listening to "CLASSICAL GAS."

Ole was having a few drinks at his favorite bar when a temperance preacher stopped to lecture him a bit. Said the preacher, "Liquor kills slowly."

"Dat's OK," said Ole. "I'm in no hurry."

■   ■   ■   ■

Ole went to a costume party and dressed himself in a Devil's costume. He was about a half mile from home when a sudden drenching rain drove him into the nearest building . . . which happened to be the scene of a revival meeting. When the congregation spotted Ole, they fled in terror . . . except for Mrs. Stensgaard who seemed transfixed by the unholy apparition. When she finally found her voice, Mrs. Stensgaard blurted, "I've been coming to dis church for tventy years . . . but I vant to tell you . . . I BEEN ON YOUR SIDE ALL DA TIME!"

■   ■   ■   ■

During a recent stock market dip, a banker lost everything. So, when Ole came around to collect a bill for some plumbing he had done, the banker explained his predicament: "I have no money to pay you, Ole, but perhaps you will accept a Rembrandt in place of money?"

"Vell," said Ole, "If it's got four good tires, you got a DEAL."

Ole and Lena took up cross country skiing and on one trip, their car stalled and they were forced to ski cross country 30 miles to get home. Telling his friend, Lars, about it next day, Ole explained how tiring it was to ski 30 miles cross country. "And to top it off," said Ole, "vhen ve got home, da first ting Lena and I did vas make love." "Vhat vas da second ting?" inquired Lars.
"Took off our skis," said Ole.

. . . .

Ole and Lena went on their first trip to San Francisco. They rode the trollies, took pictures of the Golden Gate bridge, and toured the city on a bus. Their biggest surprise was at their hotel when they opened a dresser drawer. Guess what they found? TONY BENNETT'S HEART.

. . . .

Ole picked up the rumor that Televangelist Jimmy Swaggart plans to start a magazine called REPENTHOUSE. And Jimmy Bakker allegedly has a similar idea to publish a magazine: PRAYBOY.
And, Ole says he knows a preacher who is somewhat old fashioned; he believes in the separation of Church and Motel.

OLE AND LARS' MOOSE HUNT.

Ole and Lars went moose hunting in Canada. They made arrangements for a pilot with a pontoon plane to take them in and then come back to get them. The pilot warned them not to shoot more than one moose because the plane might not be able to carry the load. Ole assured the pilot they had been able to take off the previous year with two mooses. So, when the pilot returned 10 days later, there were Ole and Lars with two moose. Reluctantly, the pilot allowed the two moose to be tied to the pontoons and the plane commenced to take off. After a shuddering take off, the plane was unable to clear the tops of the pine trees, and the plane went crashing into the side of the mountain.

After the passengers came to, Lars looked around in a daze, saying. "Where are we, Ole?" Ole replied, "Near as I can figger, ve got about 100 yards farther than we did last year."

■ ■ ■ ■

Lars and Tena invited a well-to-do Uncle for dinner. Little Arnie looked him over and finally approached the old Uncle with a request. "Uncle Knute . . . vill you make a noise like a frog for me?" said Arnie. "Vy in da vorld do you vant me to make a noise like a frog?" exclaimed the Uncle. "Because," said Arnie, "Papa says ve are going to get a lot of money ven you croak!"

Lars and Ole were visiting at Sons of Norway. "Boy," said Lars. "Every night I dream about only vun ting . . . playing baseball. Every night I go to sleep . . . and first ting I know, I'm playing baseball in my dream."

"Vell, I dream a lot too," said Ole. "Da odder night I vas dreaming dat I vas out by da seashore and two beautiful vimmen came up and started making a fuss over me. I thought about having a good time with ONE of them, but I didn't know vhat to do vid da odder vun."

"Wow!," exclaimed Lars. "Vhy didn't you get to a phone and call ME?"

"I did," answered Ole. "But they said you were out playing baseball."

■   ■   ■   ■

Ole and Lena were discussing the latest gossip regarding Mrs. Snusheim. "She didn't marry Knute for his money," said Lena, "but she sure DIVORCED him for it."

■   ■   ■   ■

Lena was getting disgusted with Ole's drinking habits. One night in exasperation, she remarked, "Ole, if you are going to drink like a fish . . . just drink what the fish drinks."

Ole had the misfortune of having his car stolen from right in front of his house. He chased the escaping car thief for three blocks until he ran out of breath. Upon reporting the theft to the police, the officer asked Ole if he could identify the thief.

"No," said Ole, "but I got the license number."

. . . .

Ole and Lena took a trip through North Dakota and crossed the Canadian border. When they got to Winnipeg, they stopped at a bank to get some Canadian currency. The bank clerk looked at the money Ole pushed through the window.

> CLERK: What denomination, please?
> OLE: Lutheran, of course.

. . . .

Ole was running his fishing boat in Puget Sound one day when he rescued a half dozen lawyers who were on a fishing trip. Sharks had been circling the scene, but they made no attempt to bother the lawyers. Mused Ole, "Must be professional courtesy."

HELGA: I vunder vhy dey took Lawrence Velk off of da TV.
LENA: I suppose because dere vas too much SAX and VIOLINS.

· · · · · ·

Little Ole was given a school assignment to write about COWS. Here is part of Little Ole's composition: "Cows have a wonderful sense of smell. You can smell them for about two miles away."

· · · ·

Ole took three copies of PLAYBOY to his elderly neighbor, Knute Starkson. Knute, who was 83, thumbed through one of the magazines and remarked to Ole, "Vell, Ole . . . bringing dis stuff to me is like giving peanut brittle to somevun after all of deir teeth have fallen out."

· · · ·

Ole and Lena had been married less than a year when Lena announced they could expect the patter of little feet. Elated at first, Ole was chagrined to learn that Lena's mother was coming to visit . . . she was a midget.

Ole turned 65 and told Lena he was going to try for Social Security. "I don't tink you can get it," said Lena. "You vere born in Norvay and you haven't got a birth certificate." Much to Lena's surprise, Ole came home with a Social Security Check.

"How in da vorld did you get dat?" exclaimed Lena.

"Very simple," answered Ole. "I yust opened my shirt collar and showed da gal da gray hair on my chest."

"Vell," said Lena, "maybe if you opened your fly, you coulda got DISABILITY."

■ ■ ■ ■

Ole was hired as a watchman for a California beach area. One day he noticed a shapely young lady sun bathing without any clothes.

"Lady," said Ole, "you can't do dat out here in public."

"I have a divine right," murmured the young beauty.

"Yah, I know," said Ole, "And the left vun ain't so bad either."

■ ■ ■ ■

Ole philosophizes every now and then. "Vhat drives me crasy sometimes," he remarked, "is how SEEDLESS GRAPES got started in da first place."

OLE: I tink da boss wants to make me part owner of da business.
LENA: Vhat makes you tink dat?
OLE: Vell, today at vork, he said, I better take an interest in da business or I'd have to look for anodder yob.

▪ ▪ ▪ ▪

Lena sent Ole down town for a bottle of liquid CHEER. He brought back a fifth of whiskey.

▪ ▪ ▪ ▪

Ole and Lars were business partners. They were at a convention in Las Vegas when suddenly Lars exclaimed, "Ole . . . Ole . . . I yust remembered dat vhen ve left da store, ve forgot to close da safe." "Nutting to vorry about," responded Ole. "Ve are both HERE, aren't ve?"

▪ ▪ ▪ ▪

Ole and Lena were visiting an art gallery seeing some of the masterpieces. Reminded by the art gallery attendant that one of Van Gogh's paintings sold for $59 million, Ole exclaimed, "Yust tink vat dat guy Van Gogh could have done if dey had "PAINT BY NUMBER" in dose days.

Ole and Lena's neighbor, Sven Carlson, went to Iowa on business. He called his wife, Helga, with some startling news: "Helga," said Sven, "I von da Iowa lottery for TWO MILLION DOLLARS. Pack your clothes."

"Vich vuns," exclaimed Helga. "Da vinter vuns or da summer vuns?"

"ALL OF DEM," answered Sven. "I vant you out of da house."

■　■　■　■

Ole and two friends, a Frenchman and an Italian, were discussing how they got their wives excited.

"I rub my wife's body with warm olive oil," said the Italian.

"I kiss my wife behind the ear," stated the Frenchman.

"Vell," said Ole, "I come home and make love to my wife and aftervard, I walk over to da drapes and use it for a towel. BOY! DOES SHE GET EXCITED!"

■　■　■　■

Ole was a bit preachy to Little Ole, trying to inspire him to ambition. He told Little Ole, "Vhen Lincoln vas your age, he vas splitting rails and vorking in a store."

Answered Little Ole, "Yah, and vhen Lincoln vas YOUR age, he vas PRESIDENT of da United States."

" WHAT'S TIME TO A PIG? "

Palmer Paulson, the Norwegian farmer, kept lifting his pig up to a tree to eat an apple. Ole, passing by, saw this and said, "Why don't you take a bunch of apples and put them in a trough? It'll save time."

"Don't be a dummy," said Palmer. "What's time to a PIG?"

. . . .

Ole was playing drums in a polka band when suddenly someone in the crowd began hurling insults at the piano player. "Who called da piano player a ##*¢%* ?" demanded Ole. A voice from the back of the room responded, "WHO called that ##*¢%* a Piano Player?"

. . . .

Ole was talking about marriage to his young nephew, Selmer. "Yah," said Ole, "Marriage is a lot like taking a bath. After you get used to it, it ain't so HOT."

. . . .

Ole was attending a lodge convention in Minneapolis. While enjoying a drink in a bar, a young lady sat on the next stool and Ole bought her a drink.Ole was enjoying the conversation, and when he asked what she did, she said she was a model.

"Are you a professional?" asked Ole.

"Well," said the young lady with a smile, "not if I like the guy."

Ole came home out of breath and puffing. He explained, "I ran behind the bus and saved 75 cents."

"Hmmph," snorted Lena. "Vhy didn't you run behind a taxi and save $2.50?"

■ ■ ■ ■

A neighbor asked Ole why the Norwegian government doesn't draft men until age 45. Explained Ole, "Dey vant to get dem right out of high school."

■ ■ ■ ■

Ole is quite a joker. On the few occasions that he takes Lena out for a nice dinner, he invariably asks the waitress, "Do you have HONEYMOON SALAD?"

WAITRESS: WHAT is Honeymoon Salad?

OLE: "LETTUCE ALONE."

(When Ole feels more daring he says, "LETTUCE . . . WITHOUT DRESSING.")

■ ■ ■ ■

Down at Sons of Norway, Ole likes to spin a few tales about his days as a sailor in the Norwegian Merchant fleet.

"Yah, I remember vell," said Ole, "Vhen a Norvegian tanker filled vid red paint collided vid a Danish tanker loaded vid blue dye. Da two ships sank and left 500 men MAROONED."

224

Sven marvelled at the agreeable way Ole got along with Lena. He asked Ole, "Vhat is your secret."
"Vell," said Ole, "I alvays tell her da truth . . . even if I have to lie a little."

. . . .

Ole met his friend Axel on the street corner and inquired about his family.

OLE: Vhere is your brudder Ingvald now?
AXEL: Oh, Ingvald is at Harvard.
OLE: Harvard? Vhat is he studying?
AXEL: He's not studying anyting . . . dey are studying HIM."

. . . .

OLE: Why don't Swedes make Kool Aid?
SVEN: I tink it is becoss it is so hard getting a qvart of vater to pour into dat little hole in da package.

. . . .

Ole Remarked, as he sat reading a magazine:
"Lena, do you know everytime I breathe, somebody dies?"
LENA: Vhy don't you try gargling vid Listerine.

225

Ole says he is grateful for soap operas and TV game shows. He says, "At least it keeps millions of vimmen drivers off da road most of da day."

. . . .

Little Ole said, "I vish I had enough money to buy an elephant." Ole responded, "Vhy vould you vant an elephant?"
LITTLE OLE: I don't. I yust van da money it vould take to buy vun.

. . . .

Lena decided that she and Ole needed a bit of culture. So they purchased tickets to the ballet. After watching the performance for 30 minutes, Ole leaned over to Lena and remarked, "I don't see vhy dey dance on their toes. Vhy don't dey yust get taller dancers?"

. . . .

Lena mentioned at a coffee party that Mrs. Nordstrom is so prudish that she blushes when someone says "intersection."

. . . .

LARS: Do you enjoy bathing beauties, Ole?
OLE: Vell, I don't know . . . I've never bathed any.

"Grandma," said Little Ole, "How OLD are you?"
"Never you mind, Little Ole," answered Grandma,
"Dare is yust some tings liddle boys shouldn't ask."
"Vell," said Little Ole, "How much do you WEIGH?"
"Now, Little Ole . . . dat's anudder qvestion you shouldn't ask your Grandma," she chided.
A few days later, Little Ole confronted his Grandma.
"Grandma," he said, "I KNOW how OLD you are. And I know how much you WEIGH. I found out from your drivers license . . . and I also found out . . .
you got an "F" in Sex."

· · · ·

Ole and Lena won a contest and the prize was a trip around the world. When they arrived in Russia, they were assigned a special guide named Rudolph. As Rudolph was showing them around Red Square, it commenced to rain a bit . . . and then some sleet came down. "Yee viss," exclaimed Ole, "Here comes da snow." "Oh no," said Rudolph the Russian, "It is RAIN!"
"And I say it is SNOW," retorted Ole.
Lena, trying to be the diplomat said, "Now, now, Ole, calm down . . . after all, Rudolph the Red knows rain, dear."

· · · ·

What is the latest use for old garbage trucks?
The Norwegians make them into campers.

227

Ole went to a Minneapolis bank to cash a check. Since Ole had no account at the bank, the clerk asked if he could identify himself.

"Sure," said Ole, "is there a mirror around here?"

"Yes," said the clerk, "on the wall behind you."

Ole moved over to the mirror, looked carefully and then turned around to announce:

"Yah, it's ME all right."

■　■　■　■

Ole is not really a good gambler. Recently in Las Vegas, while playing blackjack, he kept telling the dealer to "hit" on 20.

■　■　■　■

Lena was selected to appear on one of those Hollywood TV shows where the MC asks rather intimate questions. This is what he asked Lena:

"Which of these Shakespeare plays would you say would be most like your wedding night? "Midsummer Night's Dream," "As you like it," or "Love's Labor Lost?"

"None of dem," responded Lena. "I'd say it vas more like "Much ado about Nutting."

■　■　■　■

Why do Swedes wash their babies in Tide?
—Because it's too darn cold out 'tide.

Ole and Lena were on a trip and had a little quarrel along the way. As they passed a farm in the Ozarks, Lena spotted a Jackass grazing along a fence. Calling Ole's attention to it, she asked, "Relative of yours?"

"Of course," said Ole. "By marriage."

■　■　■　■

Ole was having some trouble sleeping, so he found a method in a magazine to help him go to sleep. So, that night he tried it out, saying: "Go to sleep little toes. Go to sleep little legs; go to sleep little arms; go to sleep little fingers." Suddenly, Lena walked into the bedroom, clad only in a filmy negligee. Ole spied her out of the corner of his eye and before he could think, he snapped his fingers and said, "ALL RIGHT! EVERYBODY UP! EVERYBODY UP!"

■　■　■　■

Jacobson was bragging to Ole as to how strong his wife was. "She can load a ton of potatoes in less than an hour," boasted Jacobson.

"Dat's nutting," said Ole. "My Lena can tie up 5 tons of copper telephone wire with her jaw for 2 or 3 hours."

■　■　■　■

Antonen, the Finn, thinks it's unlucky
to be superstitious.

229

Ole and Lena won a trip to Paris. While on a conducted tour of the famed Louvre Museum, Ole and Lena wandered away from the crowd. When they came upon the centuries-old statue of the Venus de Milo, Ole nervously grabbed Lena by the sleeve, saying, "Come on, Lena. Ve better get out of here or dey might tink ve vas da vuns who broke da arms off."

. . . . .

Ole had a bull that didn't seem to do any good when it came to breeding the cows so he called the veterinarian. The vet gave him a bottle of pills to see if it would change things. A week later, Sven came over and asked Ole about the medicine for the bull. "What kind of pills are they?" asked Sven.

"Vell," said Ole, "dey are little green pills, about da size of a bean. And (smacking his lips) dey taste something like peppermint."

. . . . .

Little Ole started Sunday school and at the first session, the teacher showed the youngsters a picture of the Christians being thrown to the lions in Rome. Then, the teacher noticed Little Ole crying . . . so she asked him what was the matter."

"Dat vun poor lion," sobbed Little Ole . . . "he ain't got no Christian."

"LET'S GET OUT 'A HERE, LENA!"

Ole ran into a bar in a strange neighborhood in Duluth and asked the bartender if he knew anything that would stop the hiccups. Immediately the bartender reached under the bar for a wet bar rag, which he slapped across Ole's face. He followed that up with a powerful squirt from a seltzer bottle.

"There. That should fix you up," said the bartender.

"Holy smoke!" exclaimed Ole. "It ain't me . . . it's LENA out in da car vid da hiccups."

■　■　■　■

Lena laughed out loud when reading the wedding column in the local paper: "This is the third marriage for the groom. He also has been through World War II."

■　■　■　■

Ole had a heated argument with Mrs. Lindstrom. Finally, in exasperation, Mrs. Lindstrom exploded: "Ole, if you vere my husband, I vould give you poison."

Not to be outdone, Ole retorted, "If you vere my vife, I'd TAKE IT."

■　■　■　■

Ole drove his old jalopy up to the toll both.

"Fifty cents," the toll collector said.

"SOLD," said Ole.

232

Ole and Lena went to a revival meeting where an evangelist was conducting a very emotional service. Working up to a fever pitch, the preacher man exhorted the crowd: "All of you who want to go to heaven, step forward. Come up to the altar."

Fifty people came forward . . . everyone except Ole and Lena.

The evangelist spotted the two hold-outs in the audience and shouted, "Don't you two want to go to heaven?"

"Sure ve do," answered Ole. "But ve didn't know you vas getting up a load to go now."

■ ■ ■ ■

When Ole came to America from Norway, he was extremely nervous when it came time to apply for citizenship. He approached the judge who gave the exam and confessed, "Yudge . . . I don't speak Englesk so purty good . . . I am yust a poor uneducated Norvegian. I'm afraid about taking da citizen testing."

"Don't you vorry, Ole . . . ve going make you a citizen of Junited States sure as my name is Yudge Bjorn Torvaldson."

■ ■ ■ ■

OLE: Why do you suppose da Indians vere here before da vhite people?

LARS: I suppose because dey had reservations.

Ole finally retired. He told the guys down at the coffee shop, "Vell, I get up in da morning vid nutting to do, and by bedtime, I'm only half-vay done."

• • • •

Ole has a T-Shirt with a rather puzzling legend:

"NO MATTER WHERE YOU GO—
WHY, THERE YOU ARE!'

• • • •

Ole got back home after a trip to Minneapolis. "Funny ting about Minneapolis. From reading their paper, I found out everyvun dies in alphabetical order up dere."

• • • •

A Swede received his draft notice and was told to bring a urine sample to the Selective Service Headquarters. Figuring on outfoxing the draft board, the Swede filled a bottle with urine from his father, girl friend, and dog, plus some of his own. After turning in the sample, the Swede waited for about a half hour. The lab technician came out to tell him: "According to our lab tests, your father has diabetes, your girl friend is pregnant, your dog is in heat, and YOU'RE in the Army."

Ole had a legal problem so he called a local attorney's office. The man who answered the phone said, "Hello, this is Swanson, Swanson, Swanson and Swanson."

OLE: Let me talk to Mr. Swanson.
VOICE: He's not here today . . . he's playing golf.
OLE: Well, then, let me talk to Mr. Swanson.
VOICE: He retired six months ago.
OLE: OK, how about putting Mr. Swanson on the line.
VOICE: Sorry . . . he's in Europe for two weeks.
OLE: Well, then, I'd like to talk to Mr. Swanson.
VOICE: SPEAKING.

■　■　■　■

Ole's cousin Selmer wanted to get to Duluth from Minneapolis, so he chose to travel by hitch-hiking. It took him THREE days because, as he explained, "I guess I must have used da wrong finger."

■　■　■　■

Ole was commenting on the way the world is today, "It's REELY sumting . . . da vay da young things go around with fancy hair-dos and skin tight pants. And da vimmen are even vorse."

Lena was telling Helga that she was determined to take off some weight. "It's getting so dat vhen I drop a dime, I have to pay a kid a nickel to pick it up for me."

- - - -

Ole was cultivating corn when Little Ole appeared on the scene.

"Papa," said Little Ole . . . "A man just came in da yard and I tink it's a preacher."

"Vell," said Ole, "Here's vhat you do. You go back and if it's a Catholic priest, you hide da wine. If it's a Lutheran preacher, hide da food. And if he's from da PTL, you sit on your mother's lap til I get there."

- - - -

Ole and Lena bought a second-hand piano. It wasn't working too well, so Lena called a piano tuner named Opper Nockity. The piano tuner worked two hours and after Lena paid him, he left. But the piano soon developed discordant sounds again and Lena told Ole the tuner should be called to come back to fix it. Ole said that he doubted the tuner would come back, because, as Ole said, "It's a vell known fact dat Opper Nockity tunes only vunce."

Ole and Lena moved to a different neighborhood. The new neighbor was a lady with six children aged one through 6. The lady told Lena that her husband had left her five years ago. "Vell," said Lena, "vhere did da odder five kids come from?"

"Oh," said the neighbor lady, "He comes back every so often to apologize."

. . . .

OLAF HARVEY, North Dakota's funniest radio personality (KFGO, Fargo) sent this dilly:

Ole's friend, Knute, can't remember where he left his expensive hat. Wandering by the Lutheran church where Sunday services were in progress, Knute steps inside the narthex. There he spots a good looking hat and considers just taking it to replace the one he lost. Suddenly, the preacher's sermon reaches his ears, and magically removes Knute's urge to steal. After the service, Knute approaches the preacher and congratulates him for a fine sermon. "You made me stop from stealing a hat to replace one I lost . . . and all because of your sermon," said Knute. "Oh . . . you mean the part about THOU SHALT NOT STEAL?" asked the minister. "No," said Knute. "It was the part about ADULTERY, and I suddenly remembered where I left my hat."

Ole went to Sears to buy some carpenter tools and decided to charge them. The credit clerk took down his name and address and then asked, "Are you a regular customer."

"Yah, I guess you could say I am," said Ole. "I take a glass of prune juice every morning."

. . . .

Ole is a little gullible. Once, at a county fair, he paid $2 to see the "Invisible Man."

. . . .

Ole and Lena had been married 50 years and a friend asked Lena, "In all those fifty years, did you ever think about divorce?"

Said Lena, "Murder yes . . . Divorce NO."

. . . .

OLE: Dat Knute Torkelson had to be da luckiest guy I ever knew.

LARS: Vhy do you say dat?

OLE: Becoss . . . he bought a $25,000 life insurance policy and died two days later. Some guys have all da luck.

Ole, just back from Minnesota reported that state has stopped painting those little airplanes in the center of the highways for air patrol surveillance. The state highway director announced that the reason was . . . that Norwegians were always trying to fly them.

■ ■ ■ ■

Ole and Lena and Little Ole were invited to a relative's home for Thanksgiving. Stuffed roast turkey was on the menu, and after dinner, Ole asked Little Ole how he liked the dinner.
LITTLE OLE: Vell, da turkey vas purty good, but I vasn't too crasy about da stuff da turkey ate."

■ ■ ■ ■

Back in the early 1900's, many hymn books combined with commercial messages as a means of reducing the cost of the books. Ole recently found one of these books which contained, among others, the following:

"Hark the Herald Angels sing . . .
Svenson's pills are just the thing . . .
Peace on earth and mercy mild . . .
Two for man and one for child . . . ."

Lena tried to explain to her neighbor, Mrs. Wentworth, what "Lace Curtain Norwegians" meant. Said Lena, "I guess you could say . . . Lace curtain Norwegians . . . are dose who have fruit in da house vhen nobody's sick."

. . . .

At one time Ole ran a dairy farm and did pretty well. He adopted a slogan which he hung on the wall:
"All dat I am . . . I owe to udders."

. . . .

Ole and Lars were in a bar watching the late evening news. A news story showed a man threatening to leap off a bridge. Ole said, "I'll bet $10 he doesn't yump." Lars said, "I'll take that bet." A few seconds later, the man jumped and Ole had to pay up.
"You darn fool," laughed Lars. "Didn't you see the SIX O'CLOCK NEWS?"
"Yah, I did," admitted Ole. "But I didn't tink da guy would be fool enough to do it again."

. . . .

Lena claims that Helga is a "suicide blonde" . . .
"dyed by her own hand."

Ole and Lena went to a nice restaurant for a change and as they were leaving, Lena helpfully suggested to Ole, "Why don't you give da girl a tip."

"OK," responded Ole. He walked over to the waitress and said, "here's a tip . . . don't stand under a tree vhen it lightnings."

. . . .

Lars Gutormson, one of Ole's old buddies, was getting feeble and was put in a retirement home. He was just getting used to the place when one of the nurses noticed Lars sitting on a bench, tipping to one side. She rushed over to straighten him up, fearing he would tip over. Soon, Lars was tipping to the other side, so the nurse hurried to straighten him again. This went on all morning. Ole came to visit Lars in the afternoon and asked how he was adjusting to the retirement home.

"Don't like it," said Lars.

"Vhy not," asked Ole.

"Becoss," said Lars, "dey von't let me lean over and pass gas."

. . . .

Ole says: Money can't buy happiness; but then, happiness can't buy groceries.

Ole was driving across Arizona when his old jalopy stalled. Hoping to find a town to get help, Ole started walking across the desolate desert. Due to the tremendous heat, Ole got disoriented and became completely lost. Nearing complete exhaustion, Ole finally came upon a blacktop road and eventually, a car stopped. "Water . . . water . . ." gasped Ole. "I gotta have water."

The motorist responded, "I don't have any water, but I have some dandy neckties I can sell you for a dollar."

"Water . . . water," gasped Ole. "I yust gotta have water."

"Well, there's a restaurant up the road about a quarter of a mile. Why don't you try them?" And with that, the motorist sped away. Summoning up his remaining strength, Ole feebly crawled the quarter mile to the restaurant. As he dragged himself through the door, he was greeted by a uniformed waiter.

"Water!" gasped Ole. "I've gotta have water!"

"Sorry," said the waiter. "You've got to have a tie."

■　■　■　■

A Norwegian named Norlander moved to Ole's town and appeared to be well to do. Ole invited him to Sons of Norway and asked him to reveal the secret of his success. Norlander made an impressive speech about becoming a millionaire. "Vell, I yust made up my mind to vork hard, to treat people nice, and most important of all, I married a vidow vid a million bucks.

OLE: "I'VE GOTTA HAVE VATER."

Ole and Lena were planning a trip to Wisconsin so they wrote a letter to a motel they had heard about asking if it would be all right to bring their dog to stay in the motel. The motel manager answered them as follows:

Dear Friends:
You ask if it is all right to bring your dog to stay at our motel. Let me begin my answer by saying we have never had a dog steal our towels; a dog has never thrown wild parties and left spilled and broken whiskey bottles in a room. In all the time we have run the motel, we have never had a dog check in with a floozy and leave the room looking like a tornado had struck. A dog has never run out on a bill or charged long distance calls on the phones that we were left to pay for. In other words, your dog is perfectly welcome to stay here; and if your dog will vouch for YOU, then you are welcome to stay here too."

■ ■ ■ ■

Ole went to Chicago for a convention. Feeling the urge to bring Lena a present, Ole went shopping at Marshall Fields. A helpful clerk suggested Ole buy Lena a new brassiere. Since Ole didn't know her size, he called her on the phone and mentioned the gift idea. "How much does da brassiere cost?" asked Lena.
"Fifteen dollars and a quarter," said Ole.
"Vell," said Lena, "You better bring me da money instead. I'M FLAT BUSTED."

244

Little Ole was getting to the age where he thought he should have a car. Ole resisted, saying he might reconsider if Little Ole would get a haircut, get better grades in school, and read the Bible every day. To Ole's surprise, Little Ole began getting straight A's. And he was reading the Bible every day. But he persisted in wearing his hair long. When asked about the promise of a car, Ole reminded him of the long hair.

"But Papa," said Little Ole, "da Bible says Jesus and all those apostles wore deir hair long.

"Yah," said Ole, "and you vill also notice the bible says dey VALKED VHEREVER DEY VENT."

■ ■ ■ ■

Lena went to the doctor for a check-up. The doctor said there seemed to be a slight heart problem and advised her to take some pills for two weeks and then come back.

"Most of all, don't climb any stairs," advised the doctor.

"Ve have a two story house," protested Lena.

"Well, I understand that," said the doctor, "but it's important that you don't climb any stairs."

Two weeks later, Lena came back and the doctor pronounced her hale and healthy.

"Can I climb stairs again?" asked Lena.

"Of course," answered the doctor.

"Good," said Lena, "becoss I vas getting tired of climbing up dat drainpipe every night."

Lundquist the Swede was talking down at the corner bar about the difference between the Italian Mafia and the Norwegian Mafia.

"The Italian Mafia makes you an offer you can't refuse," said Lundquist. "And the Norwegian Mafia makes you an offer you can't UNDERSTAND."

■ ■ ■ ■

Ole saved his money for a lifetime and decided to take a vacation on a western ranch in Montana. The following conversation took place:

> OLE: Look at dat bunch of cows.
> COWBOY: Not BUNCH . . . HERD.
> OLE: Heard WHAT?
> COWBOY: Herd of cows.
> OLE: Sure, I heard of cows.
> COWBOY: No, a cow herd.
> OLE: Why should I care what a cow heard.
> I got no secrets from da cow.

■ ■ ■ ■

Home spun philosophy according to Ole:
"A wife is a person who helps you through
all da troubles you vouldn't have had
if you hadn't got married."

One night Lena told Ole she wanted him to take her to the local entertainment center to see a personal appearance of Don Johnson, one of the stars of Miami Vice. "Nuttin' doing," snorted Ole. "I vent to school vid six guys vid dat name, so I ain't paying $10 to see anudder Don Yohnson."

■ ■ ■ ■

Lena found out Ole had been fooling around so she warned him that if she caught him one more time, there would be the devil to pay. But as fate would have it, just two weeks later, Lena came home unexpectedly from a trip and found Ole with another woman. In this case, a midget. Flinging her previous ultimatum at him, Lena chastised Ole severely. Ole looked sheepish and said, "Yah, I know I promised you Lena, and I really meant business . . . but you got to admit . . . I AM trying to CUT DOWN."

■ ■ ■ ■

Ole and Lena moved to California. Returning to the Midwest for a visit, they travelled I-94 in North Dakota, then turned off on highway 85 to go to Williston. They drove about two miles and were stopped by a highway patrolman who gave them a ticket for doing 65 in a 55 mph zone.
"Heck," muttered Ole to the patrolman, "Out in California, ve change TIRES at 55."

SEVEN

more OLE & LENA JOKES

Ole hadn't been feeling well and hated to go to a doctor. Lena finally talked him into getting a physical by agreeing to get one herself. After they had both been checked over, the doctor called Lena aside and said, "I'm afraid Ole has a very serious illness. In fact, it might be fatal. There are two things that might save his life. First, you will have to fix him three home cooked meals a day for the rest of his life. And second, you must make love to him every day without fail."

Lena pondered a bit and announced, "I'll break the news to Ole."

So, she stepped across the physicians waiting room where Ole was sitting, waiting for the diagnosis.

"Ole," said Lena, "Guess what? You're gonna DIE."

Ole was riding the bus when a young lady addressed him. She said, "Would you mind giving your seat to a pregnant woman?"

Always the gentleman, Ole relinquished his bus seat. As he looked at the lady and reflected on the situation, Ole asked, "Yust how long have you been pregnant?"

The gal answered, "About 15 minutes, and am I TIRED!"

．．．．

OLE: I know how you can sell more beer in this bar.
BARTENDER: You do? How?
OLE: Try filling up the glasses.

．．．．

LENA: Uff Da, I don't know which I dread the most . . . having a tooth pulled or having a baby.
DENTIST: Well, I wish you'd make up your mind so I will know which way to tilt the chair.

．．．．

Ole reports that Lena spent two hours in the beauty salon last Tuesday.

"And," says Ole, "dat vas yust for da estimate."

Ole came home one day and found Lena in bed with another man. Furious, Ole went to the dresser drawer and reached in for his .38 pistol. He then held the gun to his head as he confronted Lena in the bed. Lena commenced laughing hysterically. "Don't laugh, voman," said Ole. "YOU'RE NEXT!"

■　■　■　■

Doctor (on the phone): Ole, I have to tell you . . . your check came back.
Ole: Vell, let me tell YOU sumting. So did my artritis!

■　■　■　■

Ole read in the paper that a skeleton was discovered recently in a house being torn down in Fargo, North Dakota. After checking around, authorities found that it was the remains of the 1956 NORWEGIAN HIDE AND GO SEEK champion.

■　■　■　■

OLE: I heard dat Knute Hegermoe got arrested for indecent exposure.
LARS: Yah . . . he vas out in public and had to count to 21.

A farm magazine reporter asked around the community whether there was a farmer in the area who was outstanding in his field. Several people mentioned Ole. So the reporter got the directions to Ole's farm. When he located the farm, sure enough. There was Ole, out standing in his field.

. . . .

Ole was hunting big game in Africa when he suddenly came screaming through the jungle.
"What's the matter?" asked the guide.
"A lion bit off my big toe," said Ole.
"Which one?" asked the guide.
"How vould I know", said Ole,
"Dose lions all look da same to me."

. . . .

Ole and Lena went on a trip to Europe. When in Ireland, they travelled on a tour bus. The bus driver was explaining, "On your left, you will see the battleground where the Irish defeated the Norwegians in the year 982." Later on, he described another battle scene: "On your right, you can see where the Irish defeated the Norwegians in 1166."
"Vait a minute," protested Ole. "Didn't da Norvegians vin ANY of da battles?"
"Not on MY bus they didn't," responded the Irish bus driver.

"...AND ONE'S HONKING DA HORN."

Ole took four of his sows to his neighbors's farm to have them taken care of by the neighbor's boar. According to legend, the pigs were supposed to eat grass the next day if the breeding "took." Three times in a row, the mission failed and Ole had to keep hauling the sows back and forth. After the fourth attempt, Ole planned to take the sows over again in the morning. He hollered downstairs to Lena to look out and see if the pigs were eating grass. She shortly called back, "No . . . none of dem is eating grass. But three of dem are in da back of the truck, and da fourth vun is in da cab honking da horn."

Ole announced to Lena that he was going down town to city hall because of something he had to see:
He had read in the paper that the Mayor was going to lay a cornerstone.

. . . .

Ole was at the rodeo watching his friend, Tex, bulldog a steer. When Tex got bowled over by the critter, Ole rushed over sympathetically, exclaiming, "You hurt BAD, Tex?" To which Tex replied between groans, "You ever heard of anybody hurt GOOD?"

. . . .

Ole's boss had been invited to Ole and Lena's for supper. As Lena was setting the table, Ole's boss casually asked Little Ole what was being served for supper. Little Ole said, "I tink it is buzzard . . . because dis morning, Mama said to Papa, "If ve are going to have dat old buzzard for supper, it might as vell be tonight."

. . . .

Lena doesn't like her neighbor, Mrs. Kjorpestad. Lena says Mrs. Kjorpestad's mother got morning sickness AFTER she was born. And she was so ugly, they diapered her FACE.

Knute Hegermoe lived in the country near Mt. Horeb, Wisconsin. He had a habit of riding his horse into town and then getting quite inebriated. One night, Ole and some friends decided to teach Knute a lesson; so when Knute went into the bar for a night of drinking, Ole and his friends put Knute's horse's saddle on backward. The next day, they saw Knute on the street and asked how he fared the night before.

"Oh," said Knute, "I had quite a time. Somebody played a dirty trick on me and cut da head off my horse; and I vouldn't have made it home if I hadn't stuck my finger in da horse's vind pipe."

■　■　■　■

Rasmus Svenson, who was considered a real Romeo, was philosophizing at the local tavern. He said, "I never thought I vould see da day vhen I had more money dan John Connelly, better morals than Jimmy Swaggart, and more vimmen dan Don Johnson."

■　■　■　■

Ole and his friends were teasing their friend Selmer Trogstad, who was a widower, for running around with younger women.

"It's dis vay," explained Selmer. "I'd much radder smell perfume . . . dan LINAMENT."

255

Ole's favorite drinking toast:
"Vhatever you vish for me,
I vish YOU double."

■ ■ ■ ■

Ole and Lena were expecting their first child. The doctor came to their little house which unfortunately didn't have electric lights. So, while the doctor prepared Lena for delivery, he had Ole hold the lantern. Suddenly the doctor announced, "Ole, you and Lena have little BOY!"

"Svell," said Ole, "I tink I'll go to da tavern and have a drink vid da boys to celebrate."

"Wait a minute Ole," said the doctor. "Here comes ANOTHER ONE! It's a GIRL!"

"Vunderful," said Ole. "Now I can go down for a beer."

"No . . . don't go yet, Ole," said the doc. "Hold up that lantern again. Here comes ANOTHER ONE!"

"Say Doc," exclaimed Ole, "do you suppose its da LIGHT dat's attracting dem?"

■ ■ ■ ■

Lena was bemoaning her family's poor economic status. Said Lena, "Elvis Presley cleared $15 million last year. And here Ole is alive and he can't even get a JOB!"

Ole and Lena's neighbor, Rasmus announced he was getting married. Rasmus was getting along in years, so Ole and Lena were somewhat surprised when Rasmus commented he intended to start another family. Ole winked at Lena and said to Rasmus, "You better take in a boarder." A few months later, Ole ran into Rasmus and asked about his new wife. "Yah, she's going to have a baby," beamed Rasmus. Said Ole, "What did you ever do about getting a boarder?" "Oh, da boarder," said Rasmus. "SHE'S PREGNANT TOO."

■ ■ ■ ■

Ole was in the Sears Roebuck store and observed a blind man come in with a seeing eye dog. Shortly the blind man started swinging the dog around his head by the dog's leash. A clerk stepped up and said to the blind man, "Can I be of help." "Oh no," said the blind man, continuing to swing the seeing eye dog. "We're just looking around."

■ ■ ■ ■

Why are people in Stoughton, Wisconsin smarter than the people in New York? Because the people in Stoughton, Wisconsin know where New York is. But the people in New York don't know where Stoughton, Wisconsin is.

Ole met his friend Pasquale on the street and they started talking about the demise of a mutual acquaintance named Teresa.

"What did she die of?" inquired Ole.

"V.D." answered Pasquale.

"V.D.?" exclaimed Ole. "Nobody dies from V.D. anymore."

"They do if they give it to Big Tony," said Pasquale.

■　■　■　■

Ole took a trip to Russia, and while in Russia was surprised to be hosted by the head Red himself, Mikhail Gorbachev. Gorby was showing Ole around Red Square in a big Russian limousine. Suddenly, Ole witnessed a Russian soldier shooting a civilian. Ole said, "Mr. Gorbachev . . . I thought you have "glasnost" over here and now I see you shooting people." Gorbachev said he was surprised, too, so he had the chauffeur drive over to the soldier to ask the reason for his act.

"You see, Comrade Gorbachev," said the soldier, "it is on account of the curfew."

"The curfew?" snorted Gorbachev. "The curfew isn't until 10 p.m. and here it is only 9."

"I know, Comrade Gorbachev," said the soldier. "But this man comes from my neighborhood and I know he couldn't possibly have made it home in only an hour."

At the Ladies' Aid, the discussion was on the question of "When does life begin?" Mrs. Knutson stated her opinion: "At birth." Mrs. Torkelson said she thought life began at conception. Lena, however, had an entirely different opinion. "Life begins," said Lena, "ven da dog dies and da kids leave home."

■   ■   ■   ■

Lars asked Ole what he was going to have for supper. "Same old ting, I suppose," said Ole. "Cold shoulder and hot tongue."

■   ■   ■   ■

Knute met Ole on the street one day. He said, "What's new, Ole?" "Vell," said Ole. "My vife yust ran off with my best friend.
I'm sure going to miss him."

■   ■   ■   ■

Our Norwegian friends down in Decorah, Iowa, have reported a break-in at the local police department. All the toilets were stolen from the police headquarters. Our Decorah source says the police have NO clues. In fact, we are told, THEY HAVE NOTHING TO GO ON.

NORWEGIAN RIDING LAWN MOWER

Lena called her friend Ingeborg for their daily chat. She remarked how Ole had acquired a new habit of taking his rod and reel and fishing in the toilet.

"Why don't you take him to the doctor?" queried Ingeborg.

"Don't have time," said Lena. "I'm too busy cleaning fish."

. . . .

Ole came home from a PTA meeting and told Lena how the school system planned to economize.

"Dey are going to have SEX EDUCATION and DRIVERS EDUCATION . . . use da SAME CAR," explained Ole.

. . . .

Ole chopped wood for five hours for the Lutheran preacher. When he finished, he rang the doorbell at the parsonage so he could be paid. The preacher, seeking a bit of sympathy, said, "I hope you don't charge a lot, Ole . . . you see, I am just a poor preacher."

"Yah, I know," said Ole. "I've heard you preach."

. . . .

Ole started a new job, selling a line of jock straps called "Barttles and Jaymes."

Their slogan, "Thank you for your support."

Ole was sent to prison on a hold up charge. The authorities were convinced Ole had some guns hidden somewhere, but they could get no information from him.

Come spring, Lena wrote and asked when she should plant potatoes. Ole wrote back, telling her to wait a bit. A couple of weeks later, Ole wrote to Lena, saying, "The guns are buried in the back yard where we used to plant potatoes." Naturally, the mail was censored, and the authorities dug up every inch of Ole's back yard. But, to no avail. Then, a couple of days later, Ole wrote to Lena again: "NOW . . . plant the potatoes."

▪   ▪   ▪   ▪

Little Ole was called on in school to recite the pledge of allegiance. This is the way Little Ole interpreted it:

"I pledge allegiance to da flag and to the Republicans for Richard Stands. Vun naked individual vid liberty and yustice for all."

▪   ▪   ▪   ▪

Ole was drinking double shots of whiskey; every so often he would pull out a picture of Lena. Lars asked what the deal was and Ole said that after drinking double whiskies for a few hours, when Lena's picture started looking good to him, he knew it was time to quit drinking and go home.

Ole applied for a job as a watchman at the railroad yard where two rail lines intersected. The foreman doing the hiring asked Ole some questions to determine whether he was alert enough. "Ole, what would you do if you were on the job and two trains were coming toward the junction at the same time?"

Said Ole, "I vould immediately call my brudder."

FOREMAN: Call your brother? What in the world for?

OLE: 'Cause my brudder ain't never seen no train wreck before.

■ ■ ■ ■

OLE: I keep seeing spots before my eyes.

LARS: Have you seen a doctor?

OLE: No. Yust spots.

■ ■ ■ ■

Little Ole was getting to the smart aleck stage. Just before Christmas, the teacher gave the class a quiz. Little Ole turned in a blank sheet of paper across which he scrawled, "Only God knows the answers to all these questions. Merry Christmas."

His teacher's reply, written across the top of the paper said, "God gets an A. You get an F. Happy New Year."

Lena was riding on an elevator back in the days when there were no push buttons to operate them . . . just an operator. Lars Pederson happened to be the operator when Lena got on. Poor Lars was trying to get the hang of starting and stopping the elevator since it was his first day on the job. With Lars at the controls, the elevator dropped through space at a dizzying speed. Lars then threw on the brake and brought the car to a shuddering halt.

"Did I stop too qvick?" asked Lars.

"Oh no, indeed," said Lena. "I alvays vear my bloomers down around my ankles."

■　■　■　■

Ole went to see the doctor about his loss of memory. The doctor made him pay in advance.

■　■　■　■

This funnybone tickler came from Loren & Meredith Gruber of KQIS-FM, Clarinda, IA.:

Ole bought Lena a new car for their anniversary. The headlight dimmer switch was located in the turn signal, so Ole pointed that out since Lena was used to the switch being in the floorboard. That night, Lena took the car to her Ladies Circle meeting. When she got home, Ole noticed the steering wheel was bent out of shape and Lena had a sprained ankle. Lena explained: "I have a heckuva time reaching da dimmer svitch vid my foot."

OLE WANTS TO BE BURIED AT SEA.

UNDERTAKER: What can we do for you?
NORWEGIAN: I vant to make arrangements for
my funeral. I want to be buried at sea.
UNDERTAKER: Why do you want to be buried
at sea?
NORWEGIAN: To get back at my vife. She said dat
vhen I died, she was going to dance on my
grave!"

Little Ole was having trouble with his arithmetic. When Great Grandpa came in the room, Little Ole said, "Grandpa, vill you help me find da common denominator?"

"Uff Da," grumbled Great Grandpa, "Dey vere looking for dat ting vhen I vas in school! Haven't dey found it yet?"

■　■　■　■

Ole calls Lena his "Melancholy Baby" because she has a head like a melon and face like a Collie.

■　■　■　■

LARS: I hear you bought a farm for yourself, Ole.
OLE: Yah, I got fifty five cows and one bull.
LARS: Is that so? You're a pretty independent man now, aren't you?
OLE: Not half as independent as that bull.

■　■　■　■

Ole and Lena took a monkey in to live with them. A neighbor stopped in and took a look at their new pet. "Yah, he even eats at the table vid us," said Ole. "And at night, he sleeps in da bed between me and Lena." The neighbor looked somewhat astonished and inquired, "But what about the smell?"

"Vell," said Ole, "he'll have to get used to it yust like I did."

SVEN: How did Lena greet you vhen you came home late from da lodge smoker last night?
OLE: Oh, she got somevhat historical.
SVEN: Don't you mean HYSTERICAL?
OLE: No . . . she got historical and brought up all my past sins.

■　■　■　■

Ole and Lena were in a bad car wreck. Since Ole died a day before Lena, he was first at the Pearly Gates. St. Peter greeted him and said, "We have to ask you one question . . . did you ever cheat on your wife when you were on earth?"

"Not even vunce," answered Ole.

"Good," said St. Peter. "You can have that Rolls Royce automobile over there to travel around heaven."

That was fine with Ole, so he took off to look things over. In the meantime, a Swede died and came to the Pearly Gates. St. Peter explained that he would have to tell how many times he had cheated on his wife while on earth. The Swede answered, "Only four times."

So, St. Peter said, "Well, in that case, you had better take that Moped over there. The Swede took off on the little two wheeler and eventually came across Ole with his big, luxurious Rolls Royce car.

"Boy," said the Swede admiringly, "you sure got a swell car. I'll bet you were really surprised."

Said Ole, "Yah, I vas surprised . . . but not half as surprised as vhen I saw Lena on a skate board."

267

Ole was on an airplane trip. His companion in the next seat was a gorgeous young woman who made Ole's heart skip a couple of beats. "Where are you going?" asked the young Miss.

"Minneapolis," said Ole.

"Same here," said the gal. "I'm going to Minneapolis to meet the man of my dreams…because I read in a magazine that the sexiest, most romantic men on earth are NORWEGIANS and AMERICAN INDIANS. By the way, what's your name?"

Said Ole shyly, "Ole Red Feather."

■ ■ ■ ■

Mrs. Helga Knakkebrod was making some snide remarks about Ole, implying he was a failure.

Lena indignantly came to Ole's defense, saying:

"Ole started life at the bottom. It yust so happened he felt comfortable there."

■ ■ ■ ■

Ole might be considered a bit gullible. Last week, he contributed $5 to a collection being taken for the widow of the Unknown Soldier.

■ ■ ■ ■

Ole recently spent some time in the hospital. He now laughingly refers to an enema as "a goose with a gush."

268

Aanenson, the wealthy milk tycoon was telling Ole about his new girl friend. "She's 30 and I'm 65. Do you tink I vould have a better chance of getting her to marry me if I tell her I'm 50."

"No," said Ole, "I tink you vould have a better chance if you told her you vas 80."

. . . .

Little Ole's teacher, Miss Heggebust, had announced her engagement to a local man. Her students apparently shared her joy because they brought her gifts. Little Thorleiv, whose dad owned a fruit store, brought her a box of oranges. Mary Tofteskov, whose parents ran a ladies shop, brought her a purse. Little Johnny Jensen whose dad had a Danish bakery, brought her some delicious Danish rolls. Little Ole, whose dad, Ole, ran a liquor store, brought a box and set it on his teacher's desk. Teacher noticed something dripping from the box, and as she excitedly worked on the strings binding the box, she touched the fluid coming from the box and tasted it. "Mmmmmmmm" said Teacher. "I'll bet your dad sent some fine French champagne or wine from his store?"

"No maam," said Little Ole. "Puppies."

. . . .

Ole has a slogan on the bulletin board at home:
"THE HURRIER I GO, THE BEHINDER I GET."

Ole and Sven were drinking beer in the tavern when suddenly the fire alarm sounded across the street.
All the volunteer firemen got up from their stools and left. When Sven started to go, Ole said, "Sven, I didn't know you vas a volunteer fireman."
"I'm not," answered Sven.
"But my girl friend's husband IS."

■ ■ ■ ■

Ole met Lars on the street. "What's new, Lars?" asked Ole. "My vife yust ran off vid my best friend."
"Your best friend?" exclaimed Ole. "I thought I vas your best friend."
"You vas," admitted Lars, "until dis guy ran off vid my vife."

■ ■ ■ ■

LENA: Ole, I am to be in da amateur theatrical.
Vhat vould folks say if I vas to vear tights?
OLE: Dey vould probably say I married you
for your money.

■ ■ ■ ■

Lena was somewhat put out with Ole last Christmas. She had hinted she could use a pot holder as a gift. So what did Ole bring her? A GIRDLE.

LENA'S FIRST PLANE RIDE.

Lena had been gathering her nerve to take her first airline flight. But when she went to the airport and bought a ticket, she stood in line at the flight insurance counter and discovered the man in line ahead of her was the PILOT.

Ole and Lena took a trip to California. When they came to the town of San Jose, Ole looked at the "Welcome to San Jose" sign and asked Lena how the name of the town was pronounced: "Is it San Ho-zee, San Ho-zay, San Jo-zee . . . or WHAT?

"I yust don't know," said Lena. "Let's stop in at this restaurant and have a cup of coffee and we'll find out."

So, they stopped the car and parked and went in for coffee. As they were being served, Ole asked the waitress, "Say, Miss, how do you say da name of dis place?"

Said the waitress, very distinctly, "D A I R Y   Q U E E N."

■　■　■　■

Ole bought a farm near Frost, Minnesota. He started out with two windmills, but shortly took one of them down, explaining, "I figger dere ain't enough vind for TWO of dem."

■　■　■　■

Ole and Lena's next door neighbor is Mrs. Fiskeland. Lena says the woman is so dumb that she thinks "El Salvador" is a Mexican refrigerator.

■　■　■　■

OLE: What do they call outhouses in Chicago?
LARS: "The Unflushables."

272

Little Ole has been acting a bit strangely, so Ole took him to a psychiatrist.

"Tell me, son," said the shrink, "How many wheels on an automobile?"

"Four," answered Little Ole.

"Very good," said the doctor. "Now . . . what is it a cow has four of and a woman has two of?"

"Legs," said Little Ole.

"And," said the doctor, "what does your father have that your mother likes the best?"

"Money" said Little Ole.

The psychiatrist turned to Ole and said, "You don't have to worry about this boy. He's SMART."

"I'll say he is," said Ole. "I missed da last two qvestions myself."

▪ ▪ ▪ ▪

Ole's friend, Selmer Westerdahl who runs a hardware store says business is so bad that even the shoplifters have quit coming in . . .

▪ ▪ ▪ ▪

Ole had been watching Johnny Carson and Bob Hope one night, and made the following observation:

"America is da only country you can go on da air and kid da politicians, and da politicians go on da air and kid da people."

Ole had been out of work. He answered an ad to be a parachute jumper at the county fair. After he was hired, he was instructed to jump when given the signal; then to pull the first rip cord. If that one didn't work, he was to pull a second rip cord.

"Vhat do I do vhen I land?" asked Ole.

"Well, you look around for a little red truck we will have positioned to pick you up," said the instructor.

So, Ole went up in the plane, then jumped out on signal. He pulled a rip cord. Nothing happened. He pulled the second rip cord. Nothing happened. As Ole plummeted toward earth, he sighed, "Vid my luck, dat little red truck von't be vaiting for me eeder."

．　．　．　．

Ole saw this sign on the highway:
$100 FINE FOR LITTERING.

As he threw a banana peel out of his car window, Ole remarked, "That's fine with me . . . I could use the hundred dollars."

．　．　．　．

An elderly couple consulted their doctor, telling him they thought they might have AIDS. When asked what gave them reason to think that they, both 80 years old, might have the disease, they replied, "We read that you can get it from annual sex."

" GOODNIGHT, SWAMP. "

Ole was telling about Lena's mud-pack beauty treatments. "Yah," said Ole, "at bedtime, I turn out da light and I say, 'goodnight, Swamp.' "

Ole became wealthy while living in Minneapolis. He travelled to Minneapolis to transact some business with a group of financiers. These gentlemen put Ole up at the classiest hotel, and even though Ole had grown quite old, they sent up a beautiful model to keep him company in his expensive room.

"What would you like most?" purred the young lady.

"A nice hot bath," Ole replied. So the gal ran a tub for him.

"What else?" asked the model.

"How about some thunder?" said Ole. So the gal obligingly chanted, "BOOM . . . BOOM . . . .BOOM BOOM . . . BOOM BOOM."

"Great," said Ole. "Now, how about some lightning?" So the young lady switched the light on and off several times."

"Wonderful. Now, I'd like some waves," said Ole. So the gal swished her hand in the water, creating waves.

Finally, the model asked hopefully, "Ole . . . don't you want to make LOVE?"

"What?" exclaimed Ole. "In a storm like THIS?"

■ ■ ■ ■

Ole chuckled about the shenanigans of the wayward preachers. Ole remarked to Lars, "Yah, in da old days, da kids would go out behind da barn and play doctor.
Now I s'pose dey go in da garage and play Televangelist."

Lena and Ole stood up for the wedding of Lars and Helga. Shortly after the wedding, the newlyweds moved away. Ole and Lena didn't see their friends for six years, and at the reunion at their home in Wisconsin, Lars and Helga showed off their five children. Helga was so proud, and as she confided to Lena: "Yah, Lena, it sure vas lucky I got married six years ago . . . becoss as it turned out, I VAS CHOCK FULL OF BABIES!"

■ ■ ■ ■

Lena got a job writing headlines
for the local paper. After one of the
churches in town burned, she came
up with this headline:
CHURCH BURNS DOWN; HOLY SMOKE.

■ ■ ■ ■

Lena was visiting on the front porch with her friend, Kari Roomegrot, when a delivery man brought a dozen roses. They had been sent by Ole. "How thrilling," said Kari. "I bet you're really thrilled to pieces."
Replied Lena sardonically, "Vell, all it really means is I suppose I'll have to spend da next veek or so vid my legs in midair."
"Vell," said Kari. "Vat's da matter . . . don't you have a VASE?"

277

Ole was cutting a hole in the ice for ice fishing. A booming voice from the skies said: "There are no fish." Ole moved to a different spot and cut again. The voice repeated, "There are no fish here."

"Is dat you, God?" asked Ole.

"No," said the voice, "I am the rink manager."

■　■　■　■

Ole thinks that a Sanitary Belt is booze
from a clean shot glass.

■　■　■　■

Ole got a tattoo on his stomach reading "Mom." When his friends asked why it was done on his stomach rather than on his chest, Ole explained: "Vell, dere is more room on my stomach; and besides, I got da 'O' free."

■　■　■　■

When Little Ole was small, Ole used to entertain him with stories, not all of which were entirely true. So, when Ole spun a yarn about the early days in Fairbanks, Alaska, when all the dogs were banned from that city, Little Ole expressed some skepticism of Ole's tall tale. "Surely," responded Ole, "you've heard of Dogless Fairbanks, Junior."

OLE: Vhy do you suppose da dogs run so fast
in Nort Dakota?
LARS: Vell, I reckon it's becoss it's so doggone far
betveen trees.

. . . .

Lena says that Ole's favorite sandwich is a BLT.
Baloney, lutefisk and torsk.

. . . .

Ole and Lena went to a lawyer to see about getting a
divorce. "How old are you folks?" asked the lawyer.
"Vell, I'm 90 and Lena is 89," said Ole.
"How come you are getting a divorce NOW?"
asked the lawyer.
Said Ole: "Ve vanted to vait 'til all da kids were dead."

. . . .

Ole was out of town on a trip and was delayed
in getting home. When he got back the next
day, Lena informed him that a burglar had
broken into the house the night before by way
of the bedroom.
OLE: Did he get anything?
LENA: He sure did. At first, I thought it was you.

279

When Lena tried to give the phone operator her phone number on a long distance call, the operator inquired, "Do you have an area code?"

"No," said Lena. "Yust a little sinus trouble."

· · · ·

Ole's friend Tony tells about his Uncle who came to the U.S. unable to speak English. Said Tony: "My Uncle made a fortune by using just three little words:

"Stick 'em up."

· · · ·

Ole bought a ticket for a flight to Chicago. He bought some flight insurance. On his way to the plane, he stepped on a scale which read his fortune. He became panicky when he read his fortune on a little card: "The investment you made today will pay off tomorrow."

· · · ·

Lena called her grocer and said, "I sent Little Ole to you for two pounds of plums and you gave him only a pound and a half."

The grocer replied, "My scales are correct, Lena. But have you weighed Little Ole?"

Ole had his car towed into town when the motor quit. He told Sven about it, complaining about the outlandish price of $35. "Dat's a big robbery, Ole," said Sven. "Yah, I know it's a yip, but I got even. I kept da brakes on all da vay back to town."

. . . .

Ole says that even though we are in the middle
of a sexual revolution, it's just his luck
to be out of ammunition.

. . . .

Ole took his five little boys to church. The preacher remarked: "Such a nice family, Ole. Looks like you got a boy every single time." "No," answered Ole. "Sometimes ve didn't even get a ting."

. . . .

Ole was golfing with his friends, Lars, Knute and Arnie. His friends noticed Ole playing with an unusual ball with a small antenna sticking out of it. He explained it was a ball that couldn't be lost because of the beeper system in it. Said Lars: "Vhere did you get it, Ole?"
Ole replied, "I FOUND it."

Ole went into Norm Blomberg's barber shop for a haircut. An acquaintance (a Swede) named Karl Blomquist sat in the next chair to have his hair cut too. Blomquist's barber finished first; he then asked Karl if he wanted some fancy hair tonic put on. But Blomquist declined, saying, "My wife always says that stuff makes me smell like I've been to a French bordello." When Ole's barber finished with him, he asked Ole if HE wanted some of the fancy hair tonic.

"Yah, go ahead. My Lena doesn't know what a French bordello smells like."

■ ■ ■ ■

LARS: My cousin Hugo has put togedder a funny car.
He took da bumper from a '68 Chevy,
he took da engine from a '72 Ford.
Den he took da body and transmission
from a '69 Buick.
OLE: Vhat did he get?
LARS: Four years vid time off for good behavior.

■ ■ ■ ■

Mrs. Sorenson had her husband's ashes in an hour glass. She commented to Lena that while he was alive, he never worked. "So, now," said Mrs. Sorenson, "He can be useful around da house as an egg timer."

OLE HAD TROUBLE WRITING
"HAPPY BIRTHDAY" ON A CAKE.

Ole, about to get married, asked his cousin what he should do on the wedding night. The cousin, a bit too reserved to be explicit, merely advised, "After you get your clothes off, just rub her stomach and say, 'I love you, I love you.' The rest will come natural."

So, after the wedding, the couple retired to their room where they disrobed. Ole remembered the instructions, so he rubbed his new bride's stomach, saying, "I love you, I love you."

"Lower . . . Lower . . . ," said the bride excitedly.

So Ole spoke again but in a much deeper bass voice, "I LOVE YOU, I LOVE YOU."

■　■　■　■

Ole and Lars travelled to Wisconsin to attend a convention. Lars caught the eye of an attractive lady so Lars was soon on the dance floor with her. They got along so well that after the dance was over, Lars spent the night with the gal. Several months later, Ole called Lars on the phone. "Lars, do you remember dat gal you danced vid in Visconsin?"

"Yah, I sure do," said Lars with a smile. "She was a nice lady."

"And did you by any chance give her my name instead of yours?" asked Ole.

"Ya, I guess I have to admit I did," said Lars sheepishly.

"Vell," said Ole, "you must haff showed her a good time because I yust got a letter from her lawyer saying she died and left me two farms and a hundred tousand dollars."

Dear Ann Landers:

I am in love with a girl from Chicago who recently got out of jail for being a call girl. She comes from a large family and was brought up in a tough neighborhood. Her father is an ex-convict and all four of her brothers have done time for extortion, murder, and hi-jacking. She has a sister who has an escort service in New York and a guy in a black Cadillac drives her to all of her appointments. Another sister lives in Wisconsin and is married to a Norwegian.

My problem, Ann, is that I am very nervous about telling my parents about my wish to marry this girl. That is why I am writing to you for advice. I am asking you whether or not you think I should tell my parents that my intended bride is related to a Norwegian?

Signed,

Frustrated ....

(The preceding was sent to Ole anonymously in the mail. We suspect it was either from a Swede, or a Finn because it was addressed to Ole with a crayon.)

EIGHT

Even more OLE & LENA JOKES

Ole took some art lessons and became adept at oil painting. He wanted to tackle something significant so he decided to paint the contestants at the chess convention being held in the town's swankiest hotel. These were very, very dedicated chess players and were prone to bragging about their chess exploits. So, Ole painted a group picture of the chess enthusiasts as they played in the foyer area of the hotel. After finishing the painting, Ole titled it: "Chess nuts boasting in an open foyer."

■　■　■　■

When Lena turned 40, Ole jokingly said, "I tink I'll trade you in for two 20's."
Scoffed Lena, "You're not WIRED for 220."

LENA: It's a long, hot summer, Ole. How about taking Little Ole to the zoo.
OLE: Nutting doing. If dey vant him, dey can come and get him.

．　．　．　．

Ole finds himself in an employment predicament. He says, "I'm too heavy for light work . . . and too light for heavy work."

．　．　．　．

Ole complained to his landlord. "Da people upstairs are so annoying! Last night dey stomped and pounded on da floor till almost midnight.
"Did they wake you up?" asked the landlord.
"No," said Ole. "Fortunately, I vas playing my tuba."

．　．　．　．

Sometimes Ole gets pessimistic. He recently was heard to remark, "Yah, if it vas raining silver dollars, I'd be standing there vid a pitchfork."

．　．　．　．

Ole and some of his chums got on a discussion of their "first time." Ole said that he was very nervous on the occasion. "I vas alone at da time," he explained.

LARS: Vhat do you call a 300-pound Svede with a razor?
OLE: Vell, personally, I vould call him SIR

■ ■ ■ ■

LARS: Ve had a crasy ting happen at our house yesterday. My vife accidentally closed da lid on da deep freeze . . . and da cat vas in it.
OLE: For gammelost sakes! Vhat did you do?
LARS: Vell, ve took da cat out . . . it had been dere for about 6 hours, and it vas stiff as a board.
OLE: So, vhat did you do den?
LARS: I took a few drops of gasoline and put on his tongue. Yeeee Visss! Did dat cat ever come to life. He yumped about 6 feet in da air and ran around da room for about ten minutes. Den he stopped.
OLE: Vas he dead?
LARS: No. Yust out of gas.

■ ■ ■ ■

Ole says that Lena's mother is obsessively neat. He says "She even puts newspapers under da cuckoo clock."

■ ■ ■ ■

Ole says: Experience is da stuff dat ven you finally get enough of, you're too old to qvalify for da yob.

Ole says he has developed "Oldtimers Disease." He explains that it is something like Furniture Disease . . . "that's when your chest falls down into your drawers."

. . . .

Lena had two pet dogs and they both died at the same time. She took them to the local taxidermist.
"Do you want them mounted?" asked the taxidermist.
Lena thought for a moment and said, "No . . . yust have dem shaking hands."

. . . .

Ole was getting absent minded. One day he poured syrup down his back . . . and scratched his pancake.

. . . .

OLE: Can you remember Christ's last words to da Norvegians?
LARS: Yah. "Stay simple until I return."

. . . .

Ole was philosophizing one day about religion. "Yah, I don't understand all of da sqvabbling about different religions. Vhy can't ve all settle down into vun big Lutheran church?"

Ole and Lena had the Torkelsons over for Lutefisk and lefse. Torkelson liked it with plenty of melted butter and pepper. Lena couldn't find the pepper, so she rummaged through the cupboard and found a container she thought was pepper. The next day Ole and Lena discovered it actually was gunpowder. So, Ole called Torkelson on the phone and told him of the mistake.

"Vell, I'm glad to find out what happened, becoss when ve got home last night, I leaned over to tie my shoe and I accidentally shot da cat."

. . . .

Ole tells us that Lena's mother came to Minnesota in a covered wagon. Ole adds, "and if you ever have seen Lena's mother, den you vould know vhy da vagon vas covered."

. . . .

Ole was getting a little absent minded. He walked up to a man at Sons of Norway who looked familiar to him, and said, "Say . . . vas dat YOU dat died . . . or vas it your BRUDDER?"

. . . .

When Ole was single, he stated that he enjoyed the right to "Life, Liberty and the Happiness of Pursuit."

Ole and Lena's daughter Katrina told the folks that she planned to marry Sven because "he makes his living with his pen." Ole and Lena thought that must mean he is an author or journalist. As it turned out, he raises pigs.

■　■　■　■

LARS: Boy, it's raining cats and dogs.
OLE: Yah, I know. I yust stepped in a poodle.

■　■　■　■

Ole had a dog that learned how to play cards. His friend, Lars, commented on how remarkable that was.
"Vell, I don't know about dat," said Ole.
"Every time he gets a good hand, he vags his tail."

■　■　■　■

Times were tough so Ole decided to try his hand at painting. He was hired to paint the Lutheran church and he was doing well until he reached the steeple; at that point, he was running low on paint. So, Ole decided to make the paint last by thinning it out with some turpentine. As he neared the top of the steeple, he witnessed a flash of lightning and rolling thunder, accompanied by a voice from the heavens:
"OLE . . . OLE . . . REPAINT . . . AND THIN NO MORE."

Ole rushed home with good news.
"Lena . . . I yust found a great yob . . .
good salary . . . free health and life insurance,
and plenty of coffee breaks."
"Wonderful," exclaimed Lena, "I'm proud of you.
Vhen does it start?"
"You start Monday morning," Ole responded.

■　■　■　■

While Ole and Lena were at a dance, an attractive blonde approached Ole and made a big fuss over him. Lena looked on, and a few minutes later demanded to know who the gal was and what her intentions were. Ole squirmed uncomfortably, and under Lena's grilling, finally admitted he had a girl friend "on the side," and her name was Elsa. Lena was furious for a few minutes, but finally calmed down and figured since there was some competition, she had better pay more attention to Ole. In the meantime, Lars was having a fuss made over him by another gal. Lena happened to notice, so she asked Ole, "Who is dat gal talking to Lars?" Since he had just confessed about his own playmate, Ole thought he should confide in Lena about Lars. "Vell," said Ole, "dat happens to be Lars' girl friend."
Lena looked the gal up one side and down the other and snorted, "Vell, Ole, to be real honest vid you, I tink OURS is much cuter."

LENA: Ole, vill you love me ven my hair
has turned to gray?
OLE: Vhy not? I haff loved you tru all
da odder colors.

■　■　■　■

Ole says: It's awful to grow old by yourself.
Lena hasn't had a birthday in seven years.

■　■　■　■

Ole had been drinking much too often, so Mrs. Dahlgren
suggested that Lena rent a devil's suit and try to scare him
into sobriety. Lena thought that was a fine idea, and
rented a Devil's suit at the costume shop. The next time
Ole came home drunk, there was the Devil waiting for
him at the door.
"Who are YOU?" exclaimed Ole.
"I AM THE DEVIL," said Lena in a disguised voice.
"Vell," said Ole, "Shake hands, brother, 'cause I married
your sister."

■　■　■　■

Lena says kids are much stronger today than years ago.
Says Lena, "Thirty years ago, it took two people to carry
$10 worth of groceries. Nowdays a little kid can handle it."

295

Lena had a new baby and had to run an errand downtown. So, she took the street car, and during the ride, another passenger made a remark about the child belonging in a zoo. Lena stormed to the front of the streetcar and complained loudly about the insult from the passenger. "Now calm down lady . . . here is a refund on your fare . . ." said the motorman "and here's a banana for your monkey."

■ ■ ■ ■

Ole had an offer to appear in the centerfold of *PLAYGIRL* magazine (remember Burt Reynolds?). But, Ole declined at the last minute when he found out where they were going to put the staple.

■ ■ ■ ■

Ole was living out in Oregon and one day while in Portland his cousin showed him one of the new Apple computers. Ole was skeptical so he wrote down a question and fed it to the machine:

Question: Where is my father?

Answer: Your father is fishing off Cannon Beach.

Ole knew that wasn't right because his father had been dead for ten years. He then asked the computer the same question, only phrased differently.

Question: Where is the husband of my mother?

Answer: The husband of your mother has been dead for ten years, but your father is still fishing off Cannon Beach.

296

Ole was visiting the folks back in Norway, driving along a high mountain road where you can look down three thousand feet. All of a sudden, while going around a sharp curve, the left rear wheel started coming off. Ole tried to keep from panicking and began singing under his breath, "You picked a fine time to leave me loose wheel!"

Ole and Lena lost their dog, Ingemar.
Lars suggested they run an ad in the paper.
"Von't do any good . . . da dog can't read."

. . . .

LENA: Husbands are yust like woodfires. If you
don't vatch dem, dey go out.
BRITA: Yah, dat's right, and dey yenerally make
ASHES out of demselves.

. . . .

Lena bought a parrot at an auction after some very spirited bidding. "Are you sure dis bird talks?" asked Lena.
"Talk?" replied the auctioneer. "He's been bidding
against you for the past ten minutes."

. . . .

Ole was hired by the local paper to be the reporter for an
appearance by a prominent Lutheran minister. Before his
speech, the minister said to Ole, "When you do your
write-up, I would appreciate it if you wouldn't mention
the several anecdotes I plan to give. I may want to use
them in other speeches I plan to give here in town."
In his write-up, Ole wrote: "Reverend Hofstad told several stories that can't be repeated here."

Lena had to drive into town one day so she took the old red Buick. She decided to take an old gravel road to save a little time. All of a sudden, another car came toward her with a fat lady driving and waving her arm out the car window, shouting "PIG! PIG! PIG."

Infuriated, Lena, leaned out HER car window and shouted "COW! COW! COW!"

Ten seconds later, Lena's old red Buick hit the biggest sow in the whole state of Wisconsin and wrecked that old red Buick.

■　■　■　■

The Torgersons had some friends who had recently had a new baby . . . born, unfortunately without ears. Lena and Ole Torgerson planned to visit the couple to see the new baby; so Lena warned Ole not to mention anything about the child's lack of ears. Ole promised not to bring the subject up.

During the visit, Ole made some polite inquiries as to the child's health. "Yah, he's a wery healt'y baby," assured the mother. "Strong legs and arms, eats good, everyting like dat."

"How's his eyesight?" asked Ole.

"Eyesight is perfect," answered the mother.

"Vell, dat's good," blurted Ole, "because if he needed glasses, he vouldn't have no place to hook 'em on to."

Ole Swenson was a steady smoker and his wife had no luck in trying to get him to quit. So, she tried to shame him into it: 'Ole, Mr. Carlson down da street sure has got vill power. Mr. Carlson has qvit smoking. HE'S got vill power.

Ole snorted; "I'll show you vill power," and he immediately got out of his chair, went to the bedroom and moved all his clothes into the guest room. There for several weeks he stayed, sleeping alone. Lena Swenson took it good naturedly at first, but she missed Ole at night. Finally, one night she tip-toed to the guest room, opened the door slightly and whispered, "Ole! Ole! Mr. Carlson is smoking again!"

■ ■ ■ ■

A preacher stopped a Norwegian on the street and asked directions to the Post Office. After receiving the information, the preacher said, "By the way, I would like to invite you to come hear me preach tonight at the Lutheran church. I'll be talking about how you can get to heaven. Will you be there?"

"No vay!" exclaimed the Norwegian. "YOU can't even find your vay to da Post Office!"

■ ■ ■ ■

Lena says, "My doctor doesn't believe in acupuncture. He vould radder stick you vid his bill."

Ole answered the phone and soon hung up the receiver.
"Who vas it," inquired Lena.
"Somevun must have thought dis vas the Coast Guard,"
Said Ole, "all dey said vas, 'Is da coast clear?'"

▪ ▪ ▪ ▪

Ole was tired after driving his truck from Minneapolis to
Duluth, so he stopped at a diner in Cloquet for a snack.
There were five mean-looking motorcyclists from Hibbing
there, and they started pushing him around and poking
fun at him. When the waitress brought Ole's food, these
guys grabbed it from her and ate it. Ole didn't say a word.
He pulled a dollar from his pocket, paid his bill and
walked out. One of the cyclists said to the waitress:
"That Norwegian isn't much of a man, is he?"
Waitress: "No, and he's not much of a truck driver either.
He just ran over five motor bikes that were parked outside."

▪ ▪ ▪ ▪

Lena and her ladies' group were discussing the new minister. Lena reported that the handsome young reverend
had paid her a compliment . . . "He said I looked like a
breath of Spring."
Helga snorted and said, "Lena . . . that's not exactly da
vay he put it. Vhat he SAID vas . . . you looked like da end
of a long, hard vinter."

Ole was bragging to his buddy, Dave Strand, about what a good hunter he was. When they got to their cabin in Canada, 150 miles north of International Falls, Ole said, "You start the fire and I'll go shoot someting for supper." Ole walked into the woods only 3 or 4 minutes when he met a bear. Dropping his gun, Ole high tailed it back toward the cabin. Just as he reached the steps, he slipped and fell. The bear was running too fast to stop and skidded right in through the cabin door. Ole got up and slammed the door from outside, shouting to his buddy, Dave, "You go ahead and skin that one now and I'll run out and get us another."

■   ■   ■   ■

Ole says: "I only tell my troubles to my enemies. Dey are da only vuns who vant to hear dem in da first place."

■   ■   ■   ■

One day the Pope got a phone call. It was Christ on the other end. The Pope was overjoyed and asked the reason for such an historical event.

"I've got some good news and some bad news," said the Messiah.

"OK," said the Pope. "Let's start with the good news."

"Well, I've come back to earth."

"That is good news," exclaimed the Pope. "What's the bad news?"

"I'm calling from Trinity Lutheran," answered Christ.

"OLE! OLE! CAN YOU HEAR ME?"

Before Ole died, he promised Lena to try to contact her through a spiritualist.

Sure enough, Lena went to Madame Torkelson to arrange a seance.

"Ole . . . Ole . . . can you hear me?" asked Lena.

"Yah, Lena," came an eerie voice, "I can hear you."

"Vell, den Ole, how is it vhere you are?"

"Oh," said Ole, "It is beautiful here. The sky is so blue and da grass is so green. And the females are so filled out and beautiful."

Lena sighed, "It must be vunderful in heaven."

"Who's in heaven?" said Ole. I'm a BULL in Montana."

THE TENNIS SHOE WALTZ

Ay vas dansin' vid Lena Svenson
to da Tennis Shoe Valtz
Ven an old Svede I happened to see
Introduced him to my Lena,
and vhile dey vas dansin'
Dat Svede stole my Lena from me

Oh, I remember da night,
and da Tennis Shoe Valtz
You can't guess da pain it has cost
I have lost my liddle Lena
da night dey vas playin'
Dat beautiful Tennis Shoe Valtz

Now remember, all you Norskies . . .
if you have a Sveetheart
Yust listen to vhat I vill tell
Don't introduce her to a guy
who's of Svedish extraction
Or you'll be as sorry as H—l

Oh, my darling is so clever
I'll remember forever
When she vore a newspaper dress to a ball
Then her dress caught on fire
And burned her entire
Front page, Sport section and all . . .

Lena went to the doctor because she hadn't been feeling well. After some tests the doctor confronted Lena with the shocking news that at age 80, she was going to have a baby.

"A BABY . . . at MY Age . . . 80 years old? Impossible!"

"Well," the doctor said, "that's what the tests show and they never miss."

Furious, Lena picked up the doctor's phone to call Ole. "Ole, you old fool," she yelled, "YOU have made me pregnant!"

There was a pause on the other end of the line and finally Ole spoke hesitantly:

"Wh-wh-wh-who is dis speaking?"

■ ■ ■ ■

LITTLE SVEN: How come Grandma is reading her bible so much?

LITTLE OLE: She must be studying for her finals.

■ ■ ■ ■

A Norwegian out in Seattle had been reading about celebrities who reportedly snorted coke. So he decided to try it, feeling he might be missing something. However, he failed to do it because he couldn't get the bottle in his nose.

Ole was strolling along the beach when he noticed an elderly man sitting on a park bench, crying his eyes out. Sympathetically, Ole asked if the old man was broke. "No," answered the oldster, "I'm 90 years old and I've got 5 million dollars in the bank and investments."

"Well," said Ole, "you must be all alone in the vorld."

"No . . . that's not it," was the man's reply. "I'm married to a gorgeous gal who is only 32 years old. And we make whoopee three or four times a day."

Puzzled, Ole continued: "Vell, den, maybe you have lost all your friends?"

"No," responded the old timer, "I have a lot of friends and relatives, in addition to my beautiful wife."

"Vell," said Ole, "Vhat seems to be your problem?"

The 90 year-old answered:

"I can't remember where I live!"

■　■　■　■

Lena was out of town visiting relatives, so Ole was alone at home. A lonely widow next door had her eye on Ole and one early evening, she leaned over the fence with a seductive look in her eye.

"Ole," she said, "You've got what I want, and I've got what YOU want."

Ole looked at her for a minute, and then smiled, "You mean, YOU'VE got some snoose over there?"

When Ole died, he went to heaven. He was just getting used to the routine when he noticed a Swede being welcomed and given a huge reception. "Vhy in da vorld is dat Svede being treated so vell?" "Well," said St. Peter, "He's the first SWEDE we've ever gotten up here."

．　■　■　■

Ole went down to the newspaper office to place an ad which read: "Lost . . . one brindle terrier dog. Blind in left eye. Right front paw missing. Recently neutered. Answers to the name "Lucky."

■　■　■　■

Ole was talking to his new neighbor, Bruce Meland. Bruce asked Ole how he liked playing golf.
"Tried it once but never liked it," said Ole.
"How about fishing?"
"Tried it once but never liked it," answered Ole.
"Do you like water skiing?" asked the neighbor.
"Tried it once but didn't like it," said Ole.
Just then, Ole's little boy, Ole Jr., came out to play.
"That your little boy?" asked Bruce.
"Yup, sure is."
"Your only child, I assume," concluded the neighbor.

Ole was visiting in Astoria, Oregon with one of the natives, Skip Hauke. Said Ole, "You know, I read somewhere dat vun person out of three is crasy. He said dat if you are in a group, yust look at da guy on your right, den look at da person on your left. If dey both look OK, den it's got to be YOU! . . ."

▪   ▪   ▪   ▪

Ole was sitting in a tavern in Petersburg, Alaska. A giant of a man got up and chopped Ole on the back of his neck and said, "Karate chop from Japan."
A few minutes later, the same bozo ambled by and elbowed Ole in the ribs and said, "Judo from China."
Ole walked out of the tavern and returned in a few minutes with a brown bag. He walked up to the big brute who had attacked him and let him have it across the chops with the brown bag. As he was walking out, Ole said to the bartender, "Ven dat guy vakes up, tell him dat vas a hammer from ACE HARDWARE."

▪   ▪   ▪   ▪

Ole was working in the yard and told some workmen he hired to spread fertilizer to "put the manure here" and "put the manure there." The neighbor lady watching nearby was a bit embarrassed, and remarked to Lena: "Can't you get Ole to quit saying "manure."
Lena laughed. "Listen . . . I'm not complaining. It took me tventy years to get him to say 'manure'."

A Norwegian lawyer named Simons was being served in a fancy restaurant. "Waiter," said Simons, "Why is your finger in my soup?"

"I injured my finger today," answered the waiter, "and my doctor said to keep it in a warm place."

"Vell," snorted the lawyer, "vhy don't you put it vhere da sun don't shine?"

"I do," answered the waiter, "when I'm out in the kitchen."

Ole got rich and bought an alligator farm. He offered $10,000 to anybody who would dare to swim across a pool filled with hungry alligators. A Finn named Andy Carlson was looking at the pool when all of a sudden there was a splash and in a few seconds, Andy sprang out of the pool on the other side.

Ole said, "Congratulations, now you have $10,000. What's the first thing you're going to do?"

Andy: First, I want to get my hands on that blankety blank who pushed me in!

. . . .

Ole had been placed in a nursing home and before long, things got boring. So, Ole made a sign by hand that read: Whoopee on the bed, $20; on the chair, $10, on the floor, $5. He put the sign outside his door but nothing happened until three days later there was a rap on his door. There stood a little old lady with a $20 bill in her hand.

"Oh," said Ole, "I suppose you want one on the bed?"

"No," said the old gal. "I want four on the floor."

. . . .

COACH: OK, Ole . . . we've got to win this game. Get in that game and get ferocious.

OLE: OK, Coach . . . yust tell me what his number is.

People often wondered why Ole and Lena had so many kids. Ole explained it one day.

"You see, Lena is hard of hearing, and ve live near da railroad tracks. Every night the train wakes us up, and I usually say to Lena:

"Should ve go back to sleep or what?"

And Lena would always say: "WHAT?"

■   ■   ■   ■

Ole is getting along in years and a cute young gal is trying to sell him a one year subscription to a magazine.

"Heck, girly," said Ole, "One YEAR? I don't even buy green bananas anymore . . . and only a half a tank of gas at a time."

■   ■   ■   ■

Little Ole explained to his Grandma how to make toast.

"First," said Little Ole, "You take some bread, put it on da stove and burn it. Den you take it to da sink and scrape it."

■   ■   ■   ■

What's the last thing they do at a Norwegian wedding?
—They flush the punch bowl.

Ole's neighbor, Bjarne Heggestad, is a bachelor and one night while sipping a beer in the local tavern, a curvy young lady approached him with an intriguing offer. She said, "I'll do anything you want for $100."

"Follow me," said Bjarne. So, the gal did; and Bjarne proceeded to walk to his house on Elm Street. As they approached the house, Bjarne said, "Let's get this straight . . . you say you'll do ANYTHING I VANT FOR $100?"

"That's right," said the gal.

"OK," said Bjarne. "PAINT MY HOUSE."

■   ■   ■   ■

Little Ole was planning how to make a big haul at Christmas. Little Hjalmar next door tipped him off that he would be better off working through Jesus. So, Little Ole decided to write a letter: "Dear Jesus," Little Ole began, "if you bring me a lot of presents, I will never fight with my little sister again."

Then, he thought the better of it and started his letter over again: "Dear Jesus. If you bring me a lot of presents, I will eat all my vegetables that Ma cooks."

Again, Little Ole reconsidered, and this time he took a statue of Virgin Mary from a shelf, wrapped it in tissue, put it in a shoe box and hid it in the closet. Then he began the letter again . . . "Dear Jesus . . . you better bring me lots of presents if you want to see your mother again."

Ole and Lena went to the hospital so Lena could give birth to their first baby. As Ole waited in the lobby, the doctor came out to inform him that he had some good news and some bad news. "The good news is that you have a normal baby boy. The bad news is that it is a Caesarian." Ole started crying. "Vell, I'm glad it is a healthy baby . . . but I vas kinda hoping it vould be a Norvegian."

■   ■   ■   ■

Ole says: Lena is really somet'ing. She never lies about her age. Instead, she yust tells everyvun she's as old as me; den, she lies about MY age.

■   ■   ■   ■

Ole says: An old timer is somebody who remembers vhen "Five and Ten" stood for cents instead of dollars.

■   ■   ■   ■

Ole had been going to the doctor and on the most recent occasion, the doctor advised him to eat less, work harder, and not go on any vacations.
"Vill dat help my condition?" asked Ole.
"Well, no," admitted the doctor, "but it will enable you to pay your bill sooner."

Ole went to the doctor for a physical and came home with an electrocardiagram in the form of a long paper roll. Lena came home later, found the paper roll. Not knowing what it was, she put it on the player piano and it played "NEARER MY GOD TO THEE."

■　■　■　■

Ole explained to Lars how he had learned to swim as a very small boy.

"My papa used to take me out in da middle of da lake every day and I had to svim back."

Said Lars: "Gee whiz . . . dat's a tough way to learn to swim.

Ole: Learning to svim vasn't so bad . . . da tough part was getting out of dat SACK.

■　■　■　■

Ole tells about a car he bought
with a Norwegian transmission.
It's shiftless.

■　■　■　■

Ole explains the difference between the modern gals and the old fashioned gals.

"The old fashioned gal darns her husband's socks. The modern gal . . . socks her darned husband."

314

Ole's cousin Nels frequently complained about his health. Most people thought him a hypochondriac. When Nels died, he had the following inscribed on his tomb stone:

"I *told* you I vas sick."

. . . .

Little Ole was given an assignment in Sunday school class to draw a Christmas picture of the Christ Child and his family fleeing for Egypt. Little Ole made a crayon drawing showing the holy family on a jet plane. Ole's Sunday school teacher, Mrs. Nearman was amused and asked little Ole how the Christ child and family could have gone to Egypt by plane. Little Ole had an explanation. "Dey ver taken dere by Pontius da Pilot."

315

An Edina man named Cholly Starksen needed to build an addition on his house; so he consulted Ole who was a contractor and asked him for a bid. Ole figured his bid at $1,200. The homeowner asked Ole to break down the figures. Ole replied, $400 for labor, $400 for material, and $400 for me."

The man said he needed a couple more bids, so he next approached a Dane who said he could do the building for $2,400, explaining, $800 for labor, $800 for material, and $800 for me." Finally, Starksen looked up a Swede contractor named Swede Johnson who said he could get the job done for $3,600. When asked to explain, Swede replied, "Vell, dat's $1,200 for you, $1,200 for me, and $1,200 for dat dumb Norvegian with da low bid."

■ ■ ■ ■

Little Ole's teacher asked him to use the word EFFI-CIENCY in a sentence. Little Ole struggled with the task for a few minutes and suddenly his face lit up and he wrote on the paper the following:

"Tickle efficiency it wiggle."

■ ■ ■ ■

Ole is somewhat superstitious. He doesn't believe in working during any week that has a Friday in it.

Lena's good friend Helga had been going steady with Rasmus for 20 years. One night Rasmus remarked, "Helga . . . ve have been going togedder for 20 years. Maybe ve should get married."

"Married?" exclaimed Helga. "At OUR age, WHO vould have us?"

. . . .

Ole often tells about his poor childhood. "Ve vas so poor . . . da cat and I had to share da same sandbox. Da vorst part vas vhen he tried to cover me up.

And, food vas so scarce, sometimes all ve had vas popcorn for breakfast, vater for lunch, and for supper, ve vould svell up.

. . . .

One day when he was a lad of six, Little Ole climbed out of the swimming pool and announced to Ole and Lena, "I yust did someting in da svimming pool I vasn't supposed to do."

Several dozen people in the pool overheard the remark, and immediately climbed out. Seeing the furor he had created, Little Ole hastened to explain to his folks that the thing he wasn't supposed to do was . . . swim at the deep end.

Lena was being examined by the doctor.
"Ever been in the hospital?" inquired the doc.
"No . . . never in my life," answered Lena.
"Ever been bed ridden?" inquired the doctor.
"Yah," answered Lena with a smile, "Dozens of times . . . and tvice in a buggy."

. . . .

Johnson and Svensen were flying an airplane when the engine conked out. They decided to bail out so Johnson jumped first. His chute opened and he was sailing down with ease. Svensen jumped out but his chute wouldn't open. When he passed Johnson, quick as a flash Johnson started unbuckling his chute straps, remarking, "Oh, you vant to race, do you?"

. . . .

Ole was sick for three weeks and lost a lot of weight. Lars remarked that Ole was so thin that when he wore a red tie, he looked like a thermometer.

. . . .

Ole and Lena had a nice little mixed breed dog.
For the first three years of his life, the dog thought his name was "Down boy!"

Ole has figured out how to get rid of the garbage when the can gets too full.

He says, "I just gift wrap it and put it in the back seat of our car with the doors unlocked. Then, somebody steals it."

■　■　■　■

Lena was visiting with a friend, an unmarried lady named Katrina Rommegrot. "Did you hear dat Kari Vangsness lost anodder husband? Dat vas da fourth vun, and each vun vas cremated."

"Yah," sighed Katrina. "Some people have all da luck. Here I can't even get a man, and Kari has husbands to burn!"

■　■　■　■

Ole was sent by the government to find some missionaries who had gone to Africa. Being an expert sailor, Ole found the exact spot on the map where the missionaries were to have landed. He was met by a tribe of cannibals, one of whom could speak a little English.

OLE: I vant to find out if you have seen dese missionaries. (Showing a picture)

CANNIBAL: Yes . . . me see two moons ago.

OLE: How vere dey?

CANNIBAL: DELICIOUS!

Ole and Lena were getting along in years. One night Lena asked Ole if she could get something for him.

"Yah, Lena, how about getting me an ice cream sundae vith chocolate syrup and a cherry vith some vhipped cream on top. And be sure to write it down so you don't forget."

Said Lena, "I von't forget."

Lena was gone quite a while, and when she returned, she was carrying a ham sandwich. Exclaimed Ole, "I TOLD you to write it down. Where's the mustard?"

. . . .

Ole likes to compare Lena's mother with Abraham Lincoln. He says, "She has a full beard and wears a tall hat."

. . . .

Lena says she gets a kick out of going to reunions of her old friends.

She says, "Its real strange . . . seeing all those old faces and NEW teeth."

. . . .

Ole had his will made out in a very simple way:

"BEING OF SOUND MIND, I SPENT ALL MY MONEY"

"GET ME A CHOCOLATE SUNDAE...
BETTER WRITE IT DOWN."

JUDGE: The last time you were here didn't I tell you I didn't want to see you here again?
OLE: Yah, dat's vhat I told da cops, but dey vouldn't believe me.

■ ■ ■ ■

Ole says that Lena's mother is so fat that she needs GROUP insurance.

■ ■ ■ ■

A salesman calling on a Norwegian farmer noticed a pig in the farmyard with a wooden leg. While talking with the farmer, he asked about the pig.

"Yah, dat's a very special pig . . . saved my little boy's life ven he fell in da river. Pig ran up and sqvealed to beat da cars and I ran down and saved my little boy. Den, a few veeks ago my little girl fell into da vell and da pig ran and found me and sqvealed so I vould go see vhat vas da matter, and I vas able to save my little girl's life. So, you can see, dat is a very special pig."

The salesman had been listening with interest, but he just had to find out about the wooden leg. So, he came right out and asked about it. "Oh," said the farmer, "Yah, da wooden leg. Vell, you know, you yust don't eat a special pig like dat all at vun time.

TINA: My boy friend, Lars, has been telling everybody dat he is going to marry da most beautiful
girl in da vorld.
LENA: Oh, vhat a shame! And after all da time you haff been going vid him.

■ ■ ■ ■

Ole's cousin Magnus hadn't seen his relations for 20 years and finally he saved up enough money to make the trip to America. Ole was living in Bagley, Minnesota at the time. Lena answered the door when Magnus rang the bell. After he was admitted, Magnus whispered to Ole: "Vas dat your vife?"
"Of course it vas . . . do you tink I vould employ a maid dat ugly?," said Ole.

■ ■ ■ ■

Ole came into quite a bit of money and started putting on the dog. He had a phone installed in his car and immediately called his rival, a Swede named Lundquist. Ole called Lundquist to say, "I'm talking to you from da phone in my car." Of course, that burned the Swede and a week later, he called Ole to say: "I'm on way to California and I'm calling you from my car—hold the line, please, my other phone is ringing.".

323

Ole retired, and now he and Lena are in the "Honeydew" stage of their marriage.
Says Ole, "It's Honey, do dis, and Honey do dat."

■　■　■　■

A Dane was seen hitch hiking through the desert carrying a car door. He explained, "In case it gets too hot, I can roll down the window."

■　■　■　■

How do you identify the well-to-do Swedish bride?
—Her veil nearly covers her overalls.

■　■　■　■

A Swede and his Spanish friend, Roberto Flores, went out "on the town" one Saturday night. The Swede ended up in the hospital, having jumped from a second story window after about 15 drinks of Aquavit.
His friend, Flores, came to see him in the hospital. As the Swede lay in pain from several broken bones, the Spaniard explained that the Swede had made a boast before jumping that he could fly like a bird.
"But why didn't you STOP me?" exclaimed the Swede.
"STOP you?" answered Flores. "I was betting the other guys $20 that you could do it!"

Ole is a card. He's the kind of guy who will walk into an antique shop and say, "What's new?"

■ ■ ■ ■

Ole had to see a doctor, so he chose one who claimed to diagnose people simply by looking into their eyes. As he looked into Ole's eyes, he stated, "I believe you have a LOCKED BOWEL."

"Oh no," said Ole, "I got da diarrhea. So you're wrong."

"I'm never wrong," said the doctor. "You DO have a locked bowel. It just happens to be locked in the OPEN position."

■ ■ ■ ■

Little Ole was going through the prankish stage. It was bad enough when he put Crazy Glue in Ole's tube of Preparation H. Then, one Halloween, he tipped over the family outhouse . . . with Ole in it. The next day, Ole faced little Ole about the incident, and Ole Jr. readily admitted it. Ole than marched little Ole to the wood shed.

"But Papa," sobbed Little Ole, "I told you da troot . . . yust like George Vashington ven he chopped down da Cherry tree. HIS papa didn't punish HIM."

"No, dat's right," answered Ole, "but da difference is dat Yeorge Vashington's papa vasn't SITTING in da cherry tree at da time!"

NORWEGIAN BLESSING

May da ruts always fit da wheels of your pickup
May your ear muffs always keep out da Nort vind
May da sun shine varm on your lefse
May da rain fall soft upon your lutefisk
And until ve meet again . . . .
May God protect you from any and all unnecessary
Uff Das